BECOMING A MENTOR LEADER IN A PROFESSIONAL COMMUNITY

Karynne L. M. Kleine

Leigh Craft Hern

Nancy B. Mizelle

Dee M. Russell

Cynthia J. Alby

Victoria W. Hunnicutt

ScarecrowEducation
Lanham, Maryland • Toronto • Oxford
2003

Published in the United States of America
by ScarecrowEducation
An imprint of The Rowman & Littlefield Publishing Group, Inc.
4501 Forbes Boulevard, Suite 200, Lanham, Maryland 20706
www.scarecroweducation.com

PO Box 317
Oxford
OX2 9RU, UK

British Library Cataloguing in Publication Information Available

Library of Congress Cataloging-in-Publication Data

Becoming a mentor leader in a professional community / Karynne L. M.
Kleine . . . [et al.].
    p. cm.
 Includes bibliographical references and index.
 ISBN 1-57886-065-2 (pbk. : alk. paper)
 1. Employees—Training of. 2. Mentoring in education. 3. Mentoring
in the professions. I. Kleine, Karynne L. M., 1955–
HF5549.5.T7 B4133 2003
370'.71'5—dc21

                                            2003010849

∞™ The paper used in this publication meets the minimum requirements of
American National Standard for Information Sciences—Permanence of
Paper for Printed Library Materials, ANSI/NISO Z39.48-1992.
Manufactured in the United States of America.

Contents

Introduction

Dee M. Russell

We at Georgia College & State University (GC&SU), along with university faculty throughout this country, have been criticized in the popular media and state legislature for failing to prepare teachers for the complexities they will face in public school classrooms; yet, we have long been recognized by those knowledgeable in the field as preparing high-quality teachers. What is more, in recent years we have become even more effective with the implementation of a field-based cohort program with the unique position of a faculty "Mentor Leader" assigned to each student-cohort group. As this program has evolved, those of us who are in the midst of it have worked to define and understand the elements critical to our own success and the success of the program. *Becoming a Mentor Leader in a Professional Community* details how this group of university faculty participated in meaning making as a part of our professional development.

Writing the book is an act of agency and validation for the authors—a group of Mentor Leaders who explain their involvement in their university's flourishing and distinctive teacher education program. Central to the effectiveness and evolution of the program are the Mentor Leaders, the university faculty whose primary job is to usher a group of upper-division education majors through two years of development to produce excellent beginning teachers. This field-based cohort model of teacher education applies effective early childhood practices (Bredekamp and Copple 1997; Edwards, Gandini, and Forman

1993), middle grades practices (Beane 1993; Lounsbury 1984), and secondary school practices (Dewey 1922; Graham et al. 1999) to establish strong affiliative relationships (Noddings 1995), to use compelling teaching experiences to guide theory development (Korthagen and Kessels 1999; Korthagen and Lagerwerf 1996), to promote integration of learning through inquiry (Dewey 1922), and to learn to deal with uncertainty, ambiguity, and change (Hall and Spencer-Hall 1992; Toulmin 1990).

Relationships are intricate and ever-changing between the Mentor Leaders and their cohorts, other mentor leaders, and school-based faculty. To become and enact the role of mentor requires belief in the synergy of building relationships. This book explains these dynamic, elaborate, long-term relationships such that understandings of them could lead to successful replication by others in teaching and leadership roles.

Another component of the book illustrates the importance of long-term, intensive field placements that provide rich and complex experiences for preservice teachers. Lengthy field placements within diverse settings offer the context for compelling teaching experiences in which Mentor Leaders guide our students to engage in and make meaning from the practice as well as the culture of schooling.

Moreover, cohort students learn through inquiry to understand complexities within teaching and to discern relevant variables that can change the dynamics of learning in classroom communities. Their emergent understandings and individual development are mediated by the Mentor Leader's guidance and the cohort group's support. A key aspect of individual and community growth is exploring the intellectual and affective development found in ongoing, persistent relationships with the Mentor Leader and cohort peers. We have found that continual dialogue is the means for addressing "identity constraints" that inevitably arise when cohort students confront uncertainty, ambiguity, and change. Furthermore, the professionalism found within the Mentor Leader group is intentionally enacted by the Mentor Leaders through their contact with the cohorts so as to set the expectation that cohort members will collaborate likewise within the multiple contexts of "schooling." We have discovered that collaboration requires a willingness to question and transcend our individual boundaries by being open to "other," an intention that many of the teacher candidates have never encountered. When you are willing to do so, only then do the experiences become transformative. We see experience as a continuum wherein the individual education events contribute to the whole of understanding.

This book demonstrates that the role of Mentor Leader is demanding in a myriad of ways; however, developing a professional community of Mentor Leaders offers even more challenges. Thus, this synthesizing account is a departure from conventional teacher education wisdom. Conventional wisdom pays lip service to group interaction and team building, but true group development and collaboration demand shifts of typical paradigms regarding "academic freedom" and individuality in higher education. The collaborative culture of the Mentor Leader group is central to the success of our students, the program, and our own professional development. As a "humanist" perspective of professionalism and its impact on teacher education in postmodern times, this book is a timely offering, both nationally and internationally.

Simple History

Our dean, Dr. Janet Fields, who served as one of the first Mentor Leaders on the Dublin campus, focused her doctoral dissertation on our teacher education program. She summarized the beginnings of the program:

> The field-based teacher preparation program at Georgia College & State University (GC&SU) in Milledgeville, Georgia, was developed and implemented at the Macon Campus by a committee of university faculty and administrators in 1989. The program was initially limited to the preparation of teachers for certification in grades Pre-Kindergarten through grade five (Early Childhood Certification). The following year the program in Macon was extended to include certification for

teachers in grades four through eight (Middle Grades Certification). At this same time the program was also extended to a second off-campus site in Dublin, Georgia.

There are several identifiable and innovative aspects of the GC&SU field-based teacher preparation programs. The programs are largely field-based and interdisciplinary in approach. The teacher education course requirements were rearranged or reconfigured across and throughout the three quarters of each year to maximize interdisciplinary concepts.

The students in this program begin the field-based teacher education phase in their junior year of undergraduate study. The students are placed in groups of approximately 20 students and progress through the program together for six consecutive quarters in what is known as a *closed cohort.* (Students take all of their course work together with no other students participating.) Each quarter the students are placed with a different teacher, at a different grade level, in a different school. The students commit approximately seven hours every day to the program. One-half day is spent in the school and one-half day in college classes. The schedule is flexible, allowing for some whole-day experiences in the schools. (Fields 1999, 164)

Although this general outline persists, the program has adapted to a number of changes over the years. When the University System of Georgia converted to a semester calendar, faculty took the opportunity to redesign courses in the teacher preparation programs. The interdisciplinary combinations became a series of courses in Integrative Studies: Investigating the Natural World, Integrating Culture and Language into Teaching, Creative Expressions, and Connecting Social Studies across the Curriculum. Before requirements for middle grades certification changed, these courses were taken for several years by teacher candidates in early childhood, middle grades, and special education. They became unique opportunities for collaboration across teaching fields, and they provided rich occasions for collaboration among faculty across departments.

Fields' doctoral study examined influences on teacher candidates through the metaphor of a pentamerous flower "having floral whorls composed of five or a multitude of five members" (Fields 1999, 25). The five influences were preservice teachers' beliefs, school-based mentor (host teacher), university mentor (Mentor Leader), cohort group, and culture of the school.

Mentoring, by both the host teacher and the Mentor Leader, is a significant interaction that develops the teacher candidates' beliefs. The Mentor Leader is a distinctive role in our program. Traditionally, university mentors observe, evaluate, and challenge teacher candidates only during the final student-teacher placement, just before completion of a program. In the GC&SU program, the Mentor Leader guides the teacher candidates within a cohort group throughout the two-year program, which provides unique opportunities to promote consistent development from semester to semester, from placement to placement.

When the field-based teacher preparation programs—initiated and developed at off-campus sites—were implemented on the university's main campus in Milledgeville, Georgia, the program had new challenges that promoted some distinctive and unforeseen developments. Since three cohorts (in early childhood, middle grades, and special education) were started each year, faculty and teacher candidates collaborated in ways that were not possible at the off-campus sites where early childhood and middle grades cohorts were formed in alternate years. The increased number of faculty, along with the need for an increased number of host teachers in local public schools, required collaboration across programs. The challenges of adapting the off-campus programs meant that Mentor Leaders needed to confer to resolve problems and needed to develop consistent practice across departments and within departments, from year to year, cohort to cohort. Mentor Leaders in Milledgeville found it necessary to meet on a regular basis to resolve problems, discuss issues, and build consensus about implementing adaptations. "We had a strong sense that we were flying by the seat of our pants" (DR) and "building the ship while we were sailing it" (VH). The first years concentrated on logistics: figuring out which cohort would be placed in which schools, arranging classroom space on campus, reminding other Mentor Leaders about forms that needed to be completed, and so on. But subsequent years allowed mentor leaders to discuss more substantive issues—ones not merely resolving the logistical issues that allowed cohorts and instructors to collaborate, but ones examining the procedures that nurtured deeper and more provocative collaboration.

Communication Enlarges Our Experience

This book is one of the flowers of these mentor leader meetings. It is a flowering of communication:

> Not only is social life identical with communication, but all communication . . . is educative. To be a recipient of a communication is to have an enlarged and changed experience. One shares in what another has thought and felt . . . has his own attitude modified. Nor is the one who communicates left unaffected. Try the experiment of communicating, with fullness and accuracy, some experience to another, . . . and you will find your own attitude toward your experience changing. . . . The experience has to be formulated in order to be communicated. To formulate requires getting outside of it, seeing it as another would see it, considering what points of contact it has with the life of another so that it may be got into such form that he can appreciate its meaning. (Dewey 1916/1980, 8–9)

This understanding of communication is central to our development as a professional community of mentor leaders. Dewey's sense of our situation as an organism interacting with our surroundings carries a complex stream of consequences. As we interact, our doings and undergoings may involve little formulation: we do, we undergo, we move, we respond, we act. We may be aware of the immediate flow of our experience, without having formulated distinct aspects of that experience. Our living goes on, unreflected. But through communication, our experience becomes formulated, shared, expanded, transformed.

A smattering of statements from mentor leaders helps reveal our growing understanding of the centrality of communication in our work as Mentor Leaders:

The rich conversations with professors and other educators brought a sense of possibility for learning. . . . I was establishing the relationship between the action of the individual and the responses of the group. Learning was a social act where all participants selected roles. Feedback to the teacher candidate was given in terms of student behavior such as engagement levels with the material presented, types of questions the students asked, or body language that would indicate an individual was not involved with the possibility of learning in the room. . . . Each week, I brought the teacher candidates together to discuss their feedback as a group. During this seminar time, we not only discussed individual events of classrooms but what implication those events might have in the broader social contexts of teaching and learning. With the support of their seminar group, teacher candidates chose to reflect on their teaching as a social act and became more adept at focusing their own teaching on the learning behaviors of their students. (LCH)

My first group never did come together as a cohort. I found that there is a factor of trust that does not come initially, and may never come from cohort students, in the same way that it comes from one's own children; and building trust with adults is not any easier than building trust with young adolescents. I needed to be around other faculty members—to share ideas, to get help. I've learned that being a Mentor Leader carries with it a mantle of responsibility for the knowledge, skills, and dispositions cohort students need to possess to be effective teachers. (NM)

What I didn't know at the time was the depth of involvement, both personal and professional, between the Mentor Leader and the cohort students that would evolve. I supported each and every one of them . . . to make connections . . . to think critically. (VH)

As Mentor Leaders found occasions to share their own experiences, to listen and to respond to others, we found that we understood our own experiences differently. We saw from new perspectives, and we were stimulated to think about our situations in new ways.

The Pattern of the Book

Our book is a further development of the pentamerous flower. Each of the five chapters takes on the distinctive voice of its principal author.[1] Yet, we believe that through these unique qualities we are able to construct a vital, living organism: a professional community of teacher educators.

The first chapter establishes the institutional structure, the theoretically driven programmatic framework, and the Mentor Leaders' epistemic stances that support agency and empowerment. The professional community developed through the Mentor Leaders' acts is a confluence of structure, history, and individual purpose.

The second chapter examines affiliative relationships in the professional community. Affiliative relationships (also researched as "friend relationships") provide the social structure and support of new Mentor Leaders as they begin working to provide for the professional development of a cohort of teacher candidates. Noddings (1995) indicates that affiliative relationships embody an "ethic of care." In professional communities, caring may be translated as spending time with one another, respecting the individual, and negotiating resolution of conflicts, especially when they go against the community goals. The social structure is replicated in the student cohort, where it is encouraged to develop further. Each Mentor Leader brings a distinctive method for embodying social agency by the group; the cohort of teacher candidates interprets and replicates that modeled agency. Thereby, the structural goal (the School's Conceptual Framework—Architects of Change) is shared among Mentor Leaders and cohorts.

The third chapter uses the framework of an imaginary dialogue among Mentor Leaders and educational theorists to explore the ways that we support our teacher candidates in their ability to integrate theory and practice. Mentor Leaders willingly bear tremendous responsibility for preparing not just high-quality teachers but Architects of Change. This concept implies that our graduates leave with a level of accomplishment and ability much beyond traditional beginning teachers, and much beyond the preparation any one of us received in our teacher education programs. Because of our school's conceptual framework, we expect teacher candidates

- to be aware of the culture of their students and how that culture affects their students' learning;
- to become leaders in the workplace;
- to be advocates for effective and appropriate teaching practices;
- to understand and educate their public about effective assessment;
- to include colleagues, parents, and students when making decisions about their students' learning;
- to make good decisions for themselves professionally and in regards to the learning of P–12 students.

Promoting integration of learning through inquiry is the focus of the fourth chapter. Any professional program of study will require specific assignments to promote the goals of the program. In ours we have designed assignments specifically to engender positive change in our teacher candidates on the dimensions of reflectivity, collaboration, and commitment to teaching and learning. We are in part successful on these three fronts because in continual discourse we ask our teacher candidates to provide rationales for their actions, evidence for their claims. We are far less interested in helping them espouse a particular position as we are in having them determine a position and ascertaining why they are committed to that position. In journals, through work samples, and in class discussions, we frequently ask, "How did you arrive at that conclusion? On what are you basing this claim? Have you considered that from another position?" This strategy has the effect of advancing their intellects and cultivating a disposition of judiciousness while provoking their desire to engage in ongoing inquiry. Again, this professional practice of asking for substantiation of statements and subjecting thoughts to deep scrutiny is one modeled and expected in the Mentor Leader group as a method for resolving disequilibrium and refining teaching theory. New members are socialized to this expectation for being experimenters in education.

No matter who we are, we humans have difficulties confronting ambiguity and change. We intentionally create learning environments that will allow our candidates to dwell within transitive periods of change. Having learned in our Mentor Leader group that the disposition is critical to success in professional practice, we call to our teacher candidates' attention the uncertainty and ambiguity inherent in any situation, context, or event. Our role then is to facilitate their management of the disequilibria. Living the role of the Mentor Leader is a very ambiguous enterprise. Ironically, we note that the more successful Mentor Leaders, those who are able to bring about significant development of the teacher candidates, are those who see their students' lack of clarity as an opportunity to define their personal theories about being a professional educator.

Note

1. Names and initials have been changed for the Mentor Leaders who are not authors of this text.

References

Beane, J. A. 1993. *A middle school curriculum: From rhetoric to reality.* 2nd ed. Columbus, OH: National Middle School Association.

Bredekamp, S., and C. Copple, eds. 1997. *Developmentally appropriate practice in early childhood programs.* Washington, DC: National Association for the Education of Young Children.

Dewey, J. 1916/1980. *Democracy and education.* New York: Simon & Schuster.

Dewey, J. 1922. *Democracy and education: An introduction to the philosophy of education.* New York: Macmillan.

Edwards, C., L. Gandini, and G. Forman. 1993. *The hundred languages of children: The Reggio Emilia approach to early childhood education.* Norwood, NJ: Ablex Publishing.

Fields, J. S. 1999. Harmony, cacophony, and melody: Voices supporting and informing the practice of beginning teachers. Ph.D. diss., University of Georgia, Athens.

Graham, P., S. Hudson-Ross, C. Adkins, P. McWhorter, and M. Stewart, eds. 1999. *Teacher/mentor: A dialogue for collaborative learning*. New York: Teachers College Press.

Hall, P. M., and D. A. Spencer-Hall. 1992. The social conditions of negotiated order. *Urban Life* 11(3): 328–49.

Korthagen, F. A. J., and J. P. A. M. Kessels. 1999. Linking theory and practice: Changing the pedagogy of teacher education. *Educational Researcher* 28(4): 4–17.

Korthagen, F., and B. Lagerwerf. 1996. Reframing the relationship between teacher thinking and teacher behavior: Levels in learning about teaching. *Teachers and Teaching: Theory and Practice* 12(2): 161–90.

Lounsbury, J. H. 1984. *Middle school education: As I see it*. Columbus, OH: National Middle School Association.

Noddings, N. 1995. *Philosophy of education*. Boulder, CO: Westview Press.

Toulmin, S. 1990. *Cosmopolis: The hidden agenda of modernity*. New York: Free Press.

1

Professional Community/ Agency/Empowerment

Nancy B. Mizelle

> For education inevitably involves institutions as well as ideas to be communicated, and unshackling students . . . must therefore await the unshackling of their teachers.
>
> —Kloppenberg, *Uncertain Victory* (1986, 377)

Becoming a Mentor Leader in a professional community means that we must examine the context of our journey.

Sometimes it feels that we in the field of public education are trapped in the bottom of a deep well with a jumble of agitated would-be rescuers periodically peering into the crevasse, blocking the light, and beseeching of no one in particular that something be done about the situation. Their insistent admonitions reverberate down the well: "DO-SOMETHING . . . Do-Something . . . do-something . . ." They grow ever fainter so that only the weakest of rebukes reach us at the bottom; but reach us they do, amplifying our own apprehension. Meanwhile, we too are concerned about the situation, but any of our own attempts to solve the problem or gain ground as we inch our way out is overwhelmed by the din and clang of the ongoing distress signal. We know the would-be rescuers are alarmed, but beyond continual hand-wringing, we don't see much effort to assist us.

However, as a particular group of teacher educators, we see ourselves as powerful enough to effect change and improvement

1

in our own localized environment as well as in the arena called public schooling. We are an acculturated group who is able to work beyond the din and clang of the distress signal and who, by collaborating and reflecting upon the solutions, make headway on the very real problem of improving education. As Mentor Leaders of various teacher education cohorts at Georgia College & State University (GC&SU), we believe that individually and collectively we are able to effect the "unshackling" of our teacher candidates from their simplistic and dated philosophies; we are able to empower them to effectively make decisions to handle everyday classroom uncertainties and ambiguity.

Looking in from the outside, one might say that our confidence in our efforts is grounded in the historical mission of our institution—and certainly our history as an institution of teacher education is an important part of who we are as Mentor Leaders. But examining ourselves from within, we have come to realize that this belief in ourselves extends beyond our history to the professional community we are today. Our history grounds us, but our professional community empowers us and gives us agency.

A Professional Community Evolves

Our institution is steeped in a long tradition of preparing teacher educators, beginning in 1897 when the cornerstone for Georgia Normal and Industrial College was laid. As many other Normal Schools, it developed into a women's college with a unique school of education that concentrated pedagogical practice and learning around authentic classroom experiences in an onsite model school. When educator preparation began to examine and restructure ineffective programs in the late 1980s and early 1990s, the John H. Lounsbury School of Education moved to put in place a theoretically driven programmatic framework that was and still is unique in the way it brings together particular components for a teacher education program: two years of intensive field-based work with a regular course load of arts and science classes, as well as education classes for a cohort of teacher candidates directed by one Mentor Leader, similar to the concept of looping.

At GC&SU this unique framework can be traced back to the theoretical stances of teacher educators employed at the satellite campuses of the main college. In 1989, the satellite campuses provided for interesting experimentation—the programs were affiliated with the respected tradition of then–Georgia College, but they were considered "separate" from the main college programs. Detached geographically as well as structurally, the satellite campuses became the base for envisioning an "ideal" teacher preparation program by a group of teacher educators. Skeptics at the time may have felt that if the experimentation was unsuccessful, it could be explained away as an unfortunate effect of the location and would not affect the main campus's reputation. In retrospect, it seems that this detachment served more to support than deter the development of the new program. It allowed faculty the freedom to formulate and work out theory and innovation, supported by the safety of a solid reputation, thereby opening the way to program reform.

As the satellite program began to thrive, off-campus faculty interacted more frequently with the main-campus personnel and carried the valuable innovations with them. Recognizing the success of the field-based cohort program, the university administration insisted that the program be imported to the main campus. Some faculty resisted this mandate for wholesale adoption—even to the detriment of an obviously successful program. There were tensions, especially when the administration allowed faculty little freedom or room for interpretation. There were challenges to making the field-based program work on main campus in the way it had on the satellite campuses because there were more students and more Mentor Leaders working in the same schools—potentially six, compared to two at each of the satellite campuses. When Mentor Leaders from different programs were interacting with teachers in the same school, there were times of misunderstanding between the schools and the university and among Mentor Leaders. Simply said, "It was hard to communicate among the various Mentor Leaders; sometimes we had different impressions about what was expected or what had been said" (DR).

Out of these tensions, challenges, and problems with communications came the decision to meet as a Mentor Leader group. Looking back on these early meetings, we can see how issues of empowerment and agency were involved in the group's coming together—how the main campus faculty developed the Mentor Leader group to facilitate resistance (empowerment) and cement supportive relationships (agency). It is clearly evident that the theoretical views of individual campus faculty called for a type of agency that would build the relationships we now see as foundational for the success of the field-based cohort program. At the time, however, the Mentor Leader group viewed their meeting simply as a way "to build a common understanding of what we were doing" (DR)—a way to exchange ideas, pass on our experiences, and bring uniformity to the program. Looking primarily for a way to improve communication among those working with the field-based program on main campus, the Mentor Leader group did not envision their meetings developing into a professional community that would welcome and support the development of all Mentor Leaders, those on both the main and satellite campuses.

Our Professional Community Today

It takes a great deal of energy, wisdom, and perseverance to develop a cohort of strong and effective teacher candidates. Yet, this is the goal of every Mentor Leader and the impetus for our actions and interactions with our cohorts. Moreover, we have come to realize in the process of writing this book that it is through what we have identified as our professional community of Mentor Leaders reflected in the Mentor Leader group that we are able to achieve this goal. From its early beginning as a group for sharing ideas, the Mentor Leader group has evolved into a professional community that seeks to empower (Irwin 1996; Louis, Marks, and Kruse 1996) and extend agency to Mentor Leaders in all aspects of their work with one another and with their cohorts—via teaching, cohort interactions, placements, and developing relationships with other Mentor Leaders (Adajian 1996; Cady, Distad, and Germundsen 1998).

So what is this professional community? In current education literature, a professional community is a group of teachers engaged in ongoing efforts to improve their practice in a school that comprises shared values and vision; a focus on student learning; collaboration; shared practice; and reflective dialogue (e.g., Bryk and Camburn 1999; Hord 1997; King and Newmann 2000; Louis, Marks, and Kruse 1996). While our professional community certainly mirrors these characteristics, the fact that we are engaged in preparing teacher candidates adds another dimension to our work. Instead of just being concerned about shared values and what our mission statement means for us as teachers, for example, we have to be concerned about what our mission says to us about the way we prepare our teacher candidates to teach. Rather than just being concerned about collaboration among the Mentor Leaders, we as teacher educators must be concerned about how our collaboration with one another influences the way our cohort students participate in collaborative activities, and we must also be conscious to include such activities in their instruction. The complex and multifaceted nature of our responsibilities as Mentor Leaders thus defines our professional community. By professional community we mean a group of Mentor Leaders, some self-motivated, some selected, who come together to learn from one another and to solve problems aimed at the improving education through the development of empowerment and agency of the members. So that our cohort students develop into effective teachers, we must live and practice the characteristics that we believe define our community: a supportive environment, trust, collaboration, and a core of common values.

The relationships found in the professional community among Mentor Leaders and, by extension, the relationships built in a cohort are transactional—mutually and simultaneously affecting each other (Arhar 2002). Though it is difficult to identify a starting point for the transactional process, one logical entry point is to look at what happens when a new member comes into the group. In some cases, new members come through the traditional route of applying for an advertised position; in other cases, members are "tapped," or encouraged to apply, because others in the group recognize that they hold common values and see their potential as a Mentor Leader. New members come from different backgrounds and experiences—public schools and higher education; teachers and administrators; those who have worked with teacher education cohorts and those who have not. They also come with different expectations of our role as a "Mentor Leader"—from one who envisioned a Mentor Leader as "someone who would be with a group of students for two years" (KM) to one who understood that a Mentor Leader was "someone who would advise, teach, arrange and supervise field placements, and do some 'mothering' on occasion" (NM).

Regardless, we see that there is a predictable induction process: experienced Mentor Leaders go out of their way to invite new members in and accept them as colleagues during their transition. We create opportunities for conversation with new members. We seek them out; we anticipate their problems, and we work to explain the obvious and obscure aspects of our programs. We pass on those documents that explain our mission, and our traditions and history. We care about their success, and we encourage development of their sense of agency. We value whatever contribution new members have to make, even as beginning Mentor Leaders. We try to convey how important their job is and their unique responsibilities as a Mentor Leader in a well-respected program. We want all new members to feel confident that the Mentor Leader group will serve as a place where they can "get questions answered, bring up new concerns, and be validated in [their] attempts to be a good Mentor Leader" (KM).

In this supportive environment, we want new Mentor Leaders to begin to trust. Like those who have examined professional learning communities in public schools (Bryk and Camburn 1999), we too have found that trust is critical to relationships in our professional community. What we eventually determined is that a mutually trusting relationship with our teacher candidates is key to their development; and it is in the Mentor Leader group where Mentor Leaders model and see modeled the trust they need to develop with their own cohort groups. To model the trust that new Mentor Leaders need to develop and to help them develop trust in other members of the group, we ask them to share new teaching ideas and assignments. We also encourage them to address our Standards for Initial Certification in ways that are most appropriate for their program. We may offer suggestions for building cohort relationships, but each new Mentor Leader is given autonomy to develop those relations as he or she sees fit. Then, as experienced Mentor Leaders validate the efforts of the new Mentor Leaders in their teaching and cohort building, the group provides the energy for individuals to develop trust with and among members of their own cohort groups. The Mentor Leader group also serves as a means for day-to-day interaction among Mentor Leaders, which allows for an ongoing and interactive development of trust and the professional community. In other words, as the trust among Mentor Leaders increases, the level of professionalism in the community increases; and when the level of professionalism increases, the trust among the community members grows even more (Bryk and Camburn 1999).

Ultimately, it is in learning to trust one another with the overall success of the teacher education program that we model the trust we need from our cohort students and expect them to carry into the classroom. It is also in learning to trust one another that we have created a community where we feel comfortable extending ourselves and taking risks in our teaching. We have found that as the trust develops among members of our community, Mentor Leaders, both new and experienced, do not hesitate to try new ideas in a course or teach a course in an entirely different way (e.g., make a course a web-assisted course); they also are willing to step out of their "comfort zone" to collaborate with other Mentor Leaders on a new course. They feel empowered to work with their colleagues to create a learning community, much like a model middle grades curriculum, that will benefit their teacher candidates and ultimately the students they teach.

Just as trust defines the way we seek to interact with one another in our professional community, so too does collaboration. In our professional community we have an expectation for collaboration—

a willingness to talk and work together, a willingness to shape and be shaped by one another; an openness to negotiation and renegotiation; and a willingness to grow through the process (Dewey 1916/1997). The expectation for collaboration is so great that we have determined to describe it as the ethic of collaboration. As Mentor Leaders, we collaborate to arrange cohort trips; we develop and teach courses together; and we write together. We work to schedule classes together and around one another: sometimes we collaborate to make schedules that coincide; other times we collaborate to make schedules that are different. Mentor Leaders of juniors collaborate to arrange the introductory activities for the incoming cohorts and plan the awards night for the senior cohorts; senior Mentor Leaders collaborate on the evaluation of the seniors' assessment portfolio; and Mentor Leaders within the different programs collaborate to make course and programmatic changes. Then at times we all collaborate on issues like the Mentor Leader and student handbooks. Collaboration is indeed integral to our professional community.

As our professional community has developed and as new Mentor Leaders have continued to enter the group, we recognize that a process of induction and enculturation into our professional community has gradually evolved (Bryk and Camburn 1999). Over time a set of beliefs and values have developed that are important to the community and that need to be introduced to Mentor Leaders and perpetuated through this socialization process—ideas that support the development of better Mentor Leaders and teacher candidates. These shared values include the following.

The Ethic of Collaboration

Collaboration is not just something we do in our professional community; it is something that we believe in deeply. Going beyond working together to make our job easier, collaboration involves coming together with our different strengths to make the job we do better. It is in fact at the very heart of our understanding of professionalism and is therefore a critical concept for our teacher candidates to experience in their cohorts and include in their classrooms.

A Commitment to Reflective Practice

We as a community have adopted a reflective practice stance because we recognize the importance of reflection in improving our own practice and because we believe that our teacher candidates will best understand the nature and value of reflective practice by observing it modeled and examined in our university classrooms (Hudson-Ross and Graham 2000).

A Commitment to Assertiveness

Conflict and disequilibrium are common occurrences in education that are much more effectively addressed through assertive, rather than aggressive, behavior. Yet, the distinction between being assertive and aggressive is difficult for teacher candidates (and often Mentor Leaders) to understand and even more difficult to demonstrate. For this reason we are committed to assertiveness and to the courage and confidence inherent in exhibiting of assertive acting.

A Commitment to Sense of Agency

The John H. Lounsbury School of Education has chosen "Educators as Architects of Change" as the conceptual framework for its teacher preparation programs. Embedded throughout the framework's discussion of Architects of Change is language that relates to a sense of agency. We are told, for example, that teacher candidates "will develop a sense of empowerment which will allow them to enter their first classroom with confidence that they can make a difference in the lives of their students." To support the development of agency that should happen in different course and field experiences, Mentor Leaders are also committed to working to model a sense of agency with their cohort students and to use issues related to agency for whole-class discussions and seminars.

A Valuing of Public Education

As Mentor Leaders working in a public institution to prepare teacher candidates to work in the public school arena, we find it critical to value public education, the system, and those who work in it—not just to combat the negative attitudes of policy makers, but to model appropriate and positive dispositions for our cohort students.

A Commitment to Teacher Candidate Development

Mentor Leaders are committed to teacher education not just because it is their job but because it is something they believe in. They turn to colleagues, they read and research, and they conduct inquiry projects—all for new ideas on better ways to prepare teacher candidates to meet the needs of their diverse students and to deal with the uncertainty and ambiguity of the everyday classroom.

Initially, there is a grace period where new members are welcomed into the group and the community is accepting; then the expectation begins that they will respond to the culture of the community and embrace the community's core beliefs and values. Typically, new members have openly supported the community's values and fit into the professional community. For those who did not—either because they were not willing to change their philosophy, were not interested in the social interaction of the community, or could not manage the disequilibrium of the role of Mentor Leader—they have typically chosen to leave either the university or the Mentor Leader group.

Does this mean that Mentor Leaders are like cookies cut from the same cutter? That we all have the same philosophy of education? That we teach courses in the same way and organize cohort activities similarly? Certainly not! Unless we choose to do so. We each believe in our students and are committed to being an effective Mentor Leader, but we have different philosophies and different styles of teaching. The very nature of the different programs—early childhood, middle grades, special education, master's of arts in teaching—requires us to plan different experiences to support our teacher candidates' development. So while the new members of the community need to adopt a set of common values, the professional community neither mandates nor even suggests that all members give up their individual ideas about teaching. Instead, we have determined that it is the Mentor Leader group, our professional community, that empowers us and gives us agency; that provides sustenance, continuity, and avenues for growth that lead to the making of strong teacher candidates.

References

Adajian, L. B. 1996. Professional communities: Teachers supporting teachers. *The Mathematics Teacher* 89(4): 321–24.

Arhar, J. 2002. In *Middle school curriculum, instruction, and assessment,* edited by V. A. Anfara Jr. and S. L. Stacki. Greenwich, CT: Information Age Publishing.

Bryk, A., and E. Camburn. 1999. Professional community in Chicago elementary schools: Facilitating factors and organizational consequences. *Educational Administration Quarterly* 35: 751–82.

Cady, J. M., L. S. Distad, and R. A. Germundsen. 1998. Reflective practice groups in teacher induction: Building professional community via experiential knowledge. *Education* 118(3): 459–70.

Dewey, J. 1916/1997. *Democracy and education.* New York: Simon and Schuster.

Hord, S. M. 1997. Professional learning communities: What are they and why are they important? *Issues . . . about Change* 6(1): 1–8 (accessed at www.sedl.org/change/issues/issues61.html).

Hudson-Ross, S., and P. Graham. 2000. Going public: Making teacher educators' learning explicit as a model for preservice teachers. *Teacher Education Quarterly* 27(4): 5–24.

Irwin, J. W. 1996. *Empowering ourselves and transforming schools: Educators making a difference.* New York: SUNY Press.

King, M. B., and F. M. Newmann. 2000. Will teacher learning advance school goals? *Phi Delta Kappan* 81(1): 576–80.

Kloppenberg, J. T. 1986. *Uncertain victory: Social democracy and progressivism in European and American thought, 1870–1920.* Oxford, England: Oxford University Press.

Louis, K. S., H. M. Marks, and S. Kruse. 1996. Teachers' professional community in restructuring schools. *American Educational Research Journal* 33(4): 757–98.

2

Building Strong Affiliative Relationships

Victoria W. Hunnicutt

> If there is any center to the mystery of schools' success, mediocrity, or failure, it lies deep within the structure or organizational goals: whether or not they exist, how they are defined and manifested, the extent to which they are mutually shared.
>
> —Rosenholtz, *Teachers' Workplace: The Social Organization of Schools* (1991, 13)

From examining the context of our journey to examining ourselves and how we build relationships with and among mentor leaders, and by extension, our cohort students.

An unwritten premise binds veteran Mentor Leaders together: an equity of expertise in relationship to the goals of the School of Education, which are embodied by a conceptual framework—Architects of Change. Once you enter the realm of "Mentor Leaderhood," it is assumed by veteran Mentor Leaders that you support the conceptual framework and will work diligently to guide your teacher candidates to full understanding of the framework as you prepare them for their future teaching careers.

This conceptual framework embodies the heart of our teacher preparation program. It is built on four major premises:

1. foundation in the liberal arts
2. foundation in professional preparation

3. foundation in addressing human needs
4. foundation of dynamic leadership abilities

Our work as Mentor Leaders is a work in progress. It includes induction of new Mentor Leaders, establishing affiliative relationships within the group, encouraging affiliation to shared ideas, and continuing our affiliation with one another. Our work together connects to the conceptual framework in a myriad of ways.

To begin this chapter, it is necessary to define what we mean by *affiliation*. For the purpose of what we are about, *affiliation* means to associate oneself as a member with, or to connect oneself to, a particular group. As you will see in this chapter, our affiliation has evolved over time, and the relationship of the members of the group has changed over the years. Our relationships with our teacher-candidate cohorts and the relationships with public school faculty are also explored.

Initially, the Mentor Leaders affiliated as a community of learners. In time, as part of the process of deepening relationships through professional development, Mentor Leaders began to affiliate with particular ideas. Thus, in light of this first understanding of *affiliation*, we must look at caring, relationships, and communities; but, in light of the notion of *affiliation* to shared ideas, we will need to attend less to the building of affective personal relationships and more to the sharing of ideas, to distributed cognition, to the reciprocal and mutual making of meaning.

Beginnings: The Inception of the Mentor Leader Group

The evolution of the Mentor Leader group began as our teacher preparation program evolved from a traditional process to an entirely new way of preparing preservice teachers. The program change emanated from conversations among faculty working with early-childhood teacher candidates on two satellite campuses. The new model existed only on those satellite campuses for four years, until the department decided to implement it on the main campus in 1996. There were two pieces to the new model. One was that the teacher candidates would enter as a cohort in the fall and would remain together throughout their two years at GC&SU. No other teacher candidates would be admitted into the program until a new cohort started the following academic year. The faculty wanted the teacher candidates to become an active working group that developed a close, active relationship. The second piece of this new model was to place our teacher candidates in the field at the beginning of their junior year. They would have a maximum of four placements in different schools and different grade levels during that academic year.

The early Mentor Leaders paved the way for the rest of us as they took on the expanded role of mentor in addition to instructor. One of the major changes in the role of the instructor was that they not only taught courses to the teacher candidates, but they also placed and supervised those teacher candidates in their field placements. This entailed establishing relationships with public school faculties throughout the area, identifying prospective host teachers, and spending time in the field with the teacher candidates each week.

The teacher candidates were in the field for fifteen and a half hours a week and in class for fifteen hours a week. This change was, and continues to be, a difficult one for many teacher candidates. Traditionally, teacher candidates had been accustomed to attending classes, then having the rest of the week off to study and participate in other campus/community activities. Our teacher candidates are actively involved in the teacher preparation program on the average of forty daytime hours a week.

When the faculty implemented the model on main campus in 1996, a cadre of faculty emerged during the late 1990s. The things that seemed salient were the common experiences we shared and the meaning making we experienced while interacting with one another and our respective cohorts. We focused principally on matters of process—those things that we had to do to get our teacher candidates through the program. Scheduling, placements, orientation, ordering nametags, and other tedious but necessary tasks seemed to take up much of our time. That shared purpose, perhaps, was the one thing that bound us together, that helped us form a community of learners (Lambert et al. 1996). An additional purpose was to figure out this unique role that we had assumed—what it meant to us as instructors, what it meant to our teacher candidates, and what, if anything, it meant to the larger community within and without the university.

From these common experiences, a loosely formed collaborative environment developed. Vygotsky (1962, 1978) spoke about the role of meaning making through collaboration. He stated that people who were involved in a collaborative group continually receive information and feedback that inform their historical and cultural backgrounds. As we listened to our colleagues talk about what they were doing with their teacher candidates, members would interject additional ideas about how they were handling the same issues. As individuals processed those ideas and experiences elaborated on by colleagues, decisions were made by each individual Mentor Leader based on the needs of his or her particular cohort of teacher candidates (Lambert et al. 1996). Those decisions were then, at times, revisited during conversations, and those lessons learned were shared with other members of the group. For most of us, it was comforting and reassuring to know that we all shared similar issues of disequilibria (Piaget 1954). We were changing rapidly; everything was new and different. We were breaking new ground, and this "knowing" helped bind us closer together.

We called ourselves Cohort Leaders during the early years of our program, which evolved from the way our program was constructed. We each were assigned a cohort of teacher candidates at the beginning of their junior year. We shepherded those same teacher candidates for two years, until they graduated. We taught some of their classes, placed them in the field, and supervised those placements; we listened to their problems, encouraged them, admonished (redirected?) them when necessary, and quickly discovered that we were much more than college instructors. Our relationship with our teacher candidates was different from those of our peers in "the Academy" and from others within our school of education. Ours truly was a unique role within a unique program. This "special status," as we thought of it, served as additional motivation to make this new model of teacher preparation succeed.

In 1996, when the field-based teacher education model was moved from the satellite campuses to the main campus in Milledgeville, initiation of new Cohort Leaders was largely through informal, face-to-face interactions. We realized that we needed to be more focused about this process, so we began to meet as a whole group, at least once a semester.

> The group was essential in helping us all arrive at a consensus about what our programs could be. It helped the Milledgeville leaders find their own voice in contrast to the individuals from the off-campus sites. (DR)

We have continued these meetings, usually two per semester for the entire group, with two or more per semester for those involved in particular aspects of the program. We have matured as a group and as individuals.

During the past several years, the numbers of teacher candidates have increased, and departments implementing the model have expanded, which has caused membership to increase dramatically. Through discussions with colleagues in special education, it became apparent that the teacher candidates from both departments would benefit by working together. The faculty of the special education department soon implemented the field-based cohort model, and we began intermingling students from both early childhood and special education in certain courses. This intermingling gave the teacher candidates from both departments fresh perspectives of their roles as future teachers as they worked with one another on planning and implementing lessons in their placements. The faculty of the foundations and secondary department has also implemented the model to prepare teacher candidates for secondary education. Those particular teacher candidates have a master of arts in teaching when they graduate. We also include faculty from music, art, and physical education in the Mentor Leader group who have students in their final semester of undergraduate work. Because the number of faculty and teacher candidates has increased, we have added teacher liaison positions to help strengthen relationships between the university and the school systems.

As we grew in numbers and experience and as we continued to look at our roles and ourselves reflectively, a subtle switch took place. We began to see that what we do is more than just shepherding a group of teacher candidates through our preparation program. Aspects of both mentoring and leading weave themselves throughout what we do. To better delineate the nature of our mission as faculty, we decided to effect a name change from Cohort Leader to Mentor Leader. We felt that this more adequately described our relationship with our teacher candidates. As we have matured, so have the relationships within the group. We still have the strong affiliative relationship developed in the beginning, but other types of affiliation have emerged over the years.

Learning to Live with Diversity: Affiliation with the Community of Learners

When a new colleague assumes the role of Mentor Leader, there is a lot he or she must learn. In addition to planning for teaching the semester's courses, the Mentor Leader is responsible for shepherding a group of teacher candidates through two years of teacher preparation. This experience is brand new to the teacher candidates and to the new Mentor Leader. Where does she or he start? It seems that new members tend to start at the beginning, focusing on process, as the larger group did in the beginning. It is interesting to us that as each new faculty member enters the role of Mentor Leader, she or he moves through the same developmental sequence as the initial group. Our common task of getting them through the initial task of acclimating themselves to the position is made somewhat easier because of our experience.

From the beginning of the field-based cohort model, each Mentor Leader kept his or her own notebook of information, gathered from forerunners. This notebook usually included sample letters needed to arrange and consolidate our placements in public schools; a collection of special activities or field trips past groups had found stimulating; and so on. Over time, as our program grew, we realized that these particular notebooks could be consolidated and regularized as an important source of information for new initiates to our program. Two of the first Mentor Leaders, Janice Jackson and Lyndall Warren, oversaw the compilation of a Mentor Leader handbook. This handbook pulls together samples from other handbooks and includes checklists of activities to be completed each semester with the cohort group.

What the handbook doesn't tell you, though, is how to go about completing many of the tasks. So, the novice Mentor Leaders must call upon their colleagues for help. This task of making sense of the information contained in the handbook, with a focus on initial tasks to be completed, is one of the first pieces of the formal relationship that will develop over the next few years.

How do new Mentor Leaders accomplish the daunting task of preparing for the incoming cohort of teacher candidates? Typically, the novice Mentor Leader has been exposed to the current faculty during the search process, orientation, and scattered social gatherings. There may be personal connections between novice and veteran Mentor Leaders during the aforementioned activities, so the novice Mentor Leaders would typically begin by contacting one of the veterans with whom they feel comfortable.

Entering as a new faculty member on a satellite campus is a completely different experience than entering on the main campus. On the main campus, faculty have the luxury of participating in day-to-day conversations that tend to answer some questions before they are asked; in addition, they have more people around them to ask for help. A faculty member on a satellite campus tends to feel more isolated from the group.

When I first came to the position, I knew only one person on the faculty, Penny Smith. So, when I had questions, I would immediately call and ask her. What made my task a little more difficult than that of the other novice Mentor Leaders was that I was located on a satellite campus, and my predecessor, now the department chair and located on the main campus, felt a strong sense of ownership of the position that I was assuming. She offered me some suggestions but typically waited for me to ask questions. My feeling was that she had such a sense of ownership that she was afraid she would tell me to do things the way she did them; thus, she wanted me to make my own decisions about certain issues. The problem was that I didn't know enough to know what questions to ask, and by the time I figured them out, I was sometimes really under tremendous pressure to get the tasks accomplished.

My only other colleague on the satellite campus was new, and her teacher candidates were seniors, which gave her a totally different experience than my candidates did for me (mine were incoming juniors). Plus, I didn't have the advantage of having a Mentor Leader handbook. I believe it was still in the process of being developed.

> It was a real relief to get to know the other members of the department and the Mentor Leader group. We only met a few times that year, but, to me, the meetings were very helpful. When we met, we would talk about common experiences and help each other by listening to frustrations and offering suggestions. By the end of the first year I felt much more comfortable in my role, even though I knew that there was still a lot to learn. (VH)

Becoming a new Mentor Leader on campus presents frustrations, too. As a new colleague, Lois Brown experienced doubts and frustrations when she first arrived in our department. But, as the year progressed, she found support among Mentor Leaders, which helped her have a positive first year.

> When I began working at GC&SU, I wasn't certain what I was getting myself into. The only experience that I had teaching was in kindergarten, second grade, and third grade. I was no longer in a place where I could simply place a "frowning" face on a paper if things were incorrect, nor could I say that I was going to call the parents if the behavior was unacceptable. How was I going to teach COLLEGE KIDS? I didn't even know how to clock into work or what you did if you needed to take a sick day. I was a fish out of water.

Dr. Dee Russell and Dr. Vicki Hunnicutt were the two professors that I consider my saving grace. Without their help, I
wouldn't have returned for a second year. Dr. Hunnicutt was the
one responsible for getting me to orientation and helping me to
meet other faculty and staff. Not only would she help me
throughout the first two weeks here on campus, she would become a guiding light for the remainder of my first year. Dr. Hunnicutt and I taught developmental theory in the fall of 2001. She
virtually planned the class and helped me to understand what
was being taught. Throughout the semester she would call,
e-mail, and even come to the Milledgeville campus to check on
me. Without Dr. Hunnicutt's support and encouragement I
don't think I could have grown in this new position of my profession.

Dr. Russell was a person who put my mind to rest in times
of frustration and loss. There were many times that I didn't
know how to handle a particular situation with a student, and
he was the one who I would turn to for advice.

There were times that I entered his office with both guns
blazing, just to blow off some steam, and not once did he ever
make me feel as if he didn't have time to listen. There were
times when I entered his office that I felt completely inade-
quate as a Mentor Leader, and he would, in his very caring
manner, simply reassure me of my capabilities. To say the least,
Dr. Russell was very helpful in encouraging me. Through Dr.
Russell, I learned how to advise, counsel, teach, mentor, learn,
take on new challenges, and grow as a person.

I can honestly say that I am a much more confidant instructor at GC&SU. When I walked through the doors for the
first time I was intimidated by the "degrees" and scared due
to my lack of experience. I now know that I am considered an
equal to my peers—there is no degree that separates us. Each
one of us holds our own challenges in this profession, but we
all help one another strive to overcome those challenges; and
when those are met, we challenge our peers to face new ones.
(LB)

It is interesting to note that the same types of experiences
occur within our cohort groups as they enter the program.
This experience is totally new to them, and they don't know

where to start. They have to go through a period of induction, just like our new Mentor Leaders. It takes a while for the members of each cohort to establish relationships with one another. They are extremely unsure of themselves and what is expected of them at the beginning of their junior year. One of the first tasks that awaits a Mentor Leader is that of orienting the cohort to life in our program. Each cohort leader has a personal style of establishing rapport with the students and helping them establish a rapport with one another. This is an important phase of the program because these students are going to virtually live together for two years. They attend all classes together, work with the same host teachers, work in collaborative groups on projects, and get to know each other intimately in the process.

> As I watched my cohort on the first day of class, I noticed that they were "eyeing" each other very closely. My group of students was quite diverse: young ladies who had entered college right out of high school, but hadn't lived on campus; young single mothers; more mature ladies who had children of all ages, from infants to middle schoolers; and young adults in their mid-twenties and early thirties who had worked awhile before entering college, some with children and some with no children. They tentatively began talking with one another, and as time passed, began to relate to each other in very unique ways. They got along well as a large group, with only occasional spats, but seemed to gravitate towards those who were most like them. (VH)

Another relationship that the Mentor Leader must form is with principals and host teachers in the public schools. As a new Mentor Leader, one must visit the schools (typically the ones used by the former Mentor Leader) and forge new relationships with the principals. The Mentor Leader must establish a positive working relationship with the principal in each school to be able to communicate the expectations for the host teachers who will work with the teacher candidates. In addition, the Mentor Leader must also establish positive relationships with the host teachers within each school, making sure that they understand the role they will take when the teacher candidates arrive. This takes time and a certain amount of expertise.

Typically, principals are delighted to have teacher candidates from Georgia College & State University work in their schools. Host teachers usually feel the same way. Besides having a part in shaping the teacher candidate, the Mentor Leader provides the host teacher with an additional set of hands and eyes. Most host teachers do an excellent job of working with our teacher candidates. The Mentor Leader must continue to visit the schools and talk with the host teacher and the principal to reinforce the skills upon which the teacher candidates are working. As we visit the schools, the host teachers become more comfortable with us. At times, the host teachers begin our relationship thinking that we are coming to tell them how to do their job. That is certainly *not* the case. After we have visited the classroom several times and interacted with the host teachers—and after getting their feedback on the skills that the teacher candidate is successfully achieving and the skills where the teacher candidate still needs more work—the host teachers realize that we are there to be their partners. This realization moves the relationships between the Mentor Leaders and the host teachers to a new level, that of peers.

Of course, there are those host teachers who do not seem to be able to perform the necessary tasks required of our teacher candidates. When this happens, most Mentor Leaders meet with the host teacher (and sometimes the teacher candidate, also) to reconfirm with the host teacher the skills that the teacher candidates must work on. What happens in a classroom where the host teacher does not treat a teacher candidate as a teacher-in-training? Typically, the host teacher will use the teacher candidates as paraprofessionals, having them file papers, run off copies, cut out things for the students, construct bulletin boards, and so on. As we all know, these things are an integral part of teaching, but we do not want our teacher candidates to be limited to these activities. We have certain academic and behavioral expectations of our teacher candidates, and the host teachers must understand and be willing to allow the teacher candidate to practice the particular skills assigned.

From time to time, we must talk with the principal about the situation, if we can't resolve it on our own; and if the principal isn't successful either, then that host teacher is usually not used again. We try to avoid this scenario whenever possible, but it does happen.

As the Mentor Leader group has grown and as new members are inducted, those of us who have been involved in the process for a longer period of time may forget that the new faculty members don't have an understanding of how we came to be a group, and we don't stop to explain how a particular topic has come to the table. We often, as a group, don't offer enough guidance to new members so that they know the amount of work that comes with the position. We need to be mindful that new faculty are typically not used to working in a program such as ours. We must be honest with them about how we learned to manage our time so that we don't get burned out because working in this atmosphere is very labor intensive and can be extremely stressful if one does not exercise good time management. These issues are related in the thoughts of our members, which follow.

> The larger group does not do a good job bringing in the new folks. I notice that Marcy and Josie often have no idea what the others are talking about because they aren't filled in on the history of the problem. (CA)
>
> The most important thing for new members to be aware of is the stress. The type of stress that comes with this job is completely different from the stress of working in a public school. It is also imperative that the new member knows the time that must be put into this job to be successful. The job doesn't end at four o'clock, nor does it end on Friday. A lot of time outside the office must be put into this job. Once the new member knows all the responsibilities of the job, it will be important for him/her to learn how to manage their time so as not to burn out. Honesty is the only thing that will help a new member to stick it out. (MA)
>
> There needs to be a closer mentoring process for new Mentor Leaders. I still feel very hit-or-miss on many of my decisions because I often have no advance warning of issues or

dilemmas that are routine. In other words, I don't know they're "routine" until I'm faced with them for the first time. (MG)

These are issues we must begin to grapple with in order for the larger Mentor Leader group to survive and remain active as a support group. It will make the induction process much more effective if we can take these lessons to heart and make sure that our newer members have all the information they need so that they can make a smooth transition.

There is still a strong working relationship among members of the group. Part of the issue may be that our group relationship has transitioned from the "What are you doing?" and "What do I need to do?" phase to the more general phase of addressing different types of issues.

We noticed this relationship changed as we continued to interact with one another. It became more important, more vital to many of us. As we continued with discussions about classes, teacher candidates, "administrivia," and the labor intensity of our job, it became clear that our relationship was changing. We knew what we each had experienced as a Mentor Leader; this experience fostered a sense of reciprocity (Little 1982) in the relationships among members. We discussed the "meaning" of our group—just what *were* we? And, over a period of time, through continued conversations, we have slowly begun to make sense of our world. Little (1982) calls this the ability to "coevolve" (36), or grow together. As we interact with one another, the information we receive serves as feedback that enriches our conversations and enhances our learning. The process that we go through as a learning community evokes the sense of a trusting environment; it enables members to use information that underlies their perceptions to help us to continue to construct meaning and knowledge together; and it helps us understand how others and how we make sense of our world. By providing the Mentor Leader community, we are able to help novice Mentor Leaders broaden their horizons to include the larger picture of what is important. We help the new mentor leaders evolve from focusing on the process to issues of content and pedagogy by engaging them in professional conversations during meetings and in smaller groups. Members of our group have reinforced this enriched relationship by saying:

> By creating awareness among colleagues of what's being addressed in various classes, faculty are able to play to or play off of what is being addressed/taught in another class. (MG)
>
> Without the support of my peers I wouldn't have felt confident enough to fulfill tasks, nor would I have felt confident enough to step outside of my box and venture new roles for myself. (LB)
>
> I was focused for a long while on the mundane tasks that greet new Mentor Leaders. The interaction of the Mentor Leader group during meetings helped me transition from focusing on that process to focusing on how I was teaching and on the content. Our conversations helped me grow into thinking more seriously about how I inform and involve my students in their learning. (VH)

The evolution of the cohort group continues to follow the same path as that of the Mentor Leader group. By the end of the first semester, they are beginning to gel as a group. They support one another, encourage one another, and continue to learn to work together. The group typically has periods of adjustment, as members become more vocal and as individual personalities come to the forefront. They slowly begin to transition from being acquaintances to colleagues. If disputes develop, we let them work out the issues themselves. We have found that this autonomy helps them grow professionally in a way that is quite remarkable. Leaders begin to emerge and to take that leadership role. Others find their place within the group, and all discover that each person has something to bring to the group.

Besides interacting with individual Mentor Leaders during the beginning of the academic year, other formal relationships help us become a member of the professional community. Some of the many ways we interact with our colleagues on a regular basis include committee assignments, co-planning, and teaching, as well as faculty meetings, acclimation to the campus-at-large, and professional organizations. These interactions help us become acclimated to the structure and climate of our particular departments, even though the core of the Mentor Leader relationship spans different programs: early childhood (P–5) and middle grades (4–8); special education (P–12); and the master of arts in teaching (7–12). Professors from music education and health as well as physical education and recreation are also members of our group, even though the relationship with their teacher candidates is different from our relationship.

With the addition of these members, the focus of the larger group has had to change. We deal more now with administrative items that affect all departments. At times our discussions remain relevant to the larger group, but at other times, we deviate and tend to discuss issues that are more germane to subgroups. This pattern does become frustrating to some members of the group, which is expected. What we don't do, at certain times, is recognize that this is happening and move to table that particular discussion until only the people affected by the subject are present. When this happens, Lambert and colleagues (1996) say that members will then process the information presented within their frame of reference and become either stimulated by others' perspectives or conflicted by them. We see evidence of this in responses given by members of the group.

> I become personally fatigued with ML meetings because my working style is much different from many members of the group. Prolonged conversations about details are very tiresome to me, and I usually think that they are of little benefit compared to other tasks that could be accomplished in that time period. (MG)
>
> There are too many people in it for it to be affective to promote real transformation. It mostly serves an administrative function. Many of the conversations digress into topics that are only of interest to one group and not the others. I think the secondary Mentor Leaders, including myself, are largely frustrated with both the large group meetings and the endless e-mails. The real work happens in smaller groups. Somehow we have to narrow what the larger group does so that it is more productive. (CA)

The Beginning of Professional Development:
Affiliation to Ideas

From the beginning of the program, ideas have been important to the Mentor Leaders who have played an important role in creating this distinctive model of teacher education. In the late 1980s, the program was conceived as an alternative to a traditional program in teacher education, built from a series of courses, and ending in an extended period of student teaching in a public school classroom. *Field-based education* was the key idea that stimulated the formation of this program and that guided its early construction on satellite campuses in Macon and in Dublin. Teacher candidates were to be placed in public school classrooms throughout the two-year program; these placements were to be an integral part of their formation, serving as places where teacher candidates would be able to observe and apply the concepts that they learned in university classrooms.

As an element of this field-based program, courses were reconfigured so that teacher candidates would be more able to apply integrated curriculum units in their field placements. In the first semester, the teacher candidates had a beginning literacy course in which they planned, as a group, a literature focus unit consisting of several types of literacy lessons focused around one book. This was one of the first collaborative activities in which the cohort group participated. The following semester, they took an early childhood curriculum course and learned to plan and implement an integrated unit across all curriculum areas. As the students took these courses and practiced what they were learning in their field placements, faculty began conversations about what the students were actually gaining from these experiences. They were immersed in classrooms where they observed a variety of teaching styles, and they came back to campus full of questions about what they were doing and what they saw their host teachers doing. As time passed, this intense laboratory method became a tool for deepening the understanding of what they, as teachers, would be expected to do. The candidates were able to take the methods modeled for them by faculty and apply those same methods immediately. We began to realize that this was a powerful tool, much more powerful than having them exist within an environment that supports only demonstration.

When the field-based program in teacher education was moved to the main campus in 1996, the university was in the midst of a systemwide initiative to convert from a quarter system to semesters. All courses were being revised at this time. A new set of courses in Integrated Studies was proposed for the teacher education programs. These courses were an outgrowth of the practice of recombining traditional courses to enhance understanding of integrated curriculum. Methods courses were organized around major themes of science and social studies. The fine arts were added, and special education candidates were required to participate in a creative expressions course, where they worked with early childhood candidates to design and implement a unit that incorporated all the fine arts and was applicable to both regular education and special education students alike. From this course revamping, the desire to collaborate across departments became a key ingredient within our program.

From the beginning of the program in Milledgeville, Mentor Leaders planned together. They planned an orientation to the program that involved teacher candidates in all programs, and they planned and taught courses together. At first, these were only the courses in Integrative Studies, but as time passed and as the numbers grew, instructors teaching sections of the same course conferred. This collaboration on the main campus was new to the field-based program, as it had been implemented on the satellite campuses, where single directors had worked alone. Mentor Leaders on the main campus tried to help those on the satellite campuses to work more collaboratively, not only to make sure that courses were similar, but also out of a growing conviction that such collaboration widened our own understanding of the material, strengthened our abilities to teach effectively, and exposed our teacher candidates to multiple perspectives.

We began to work more closely together in the classroom. The number of classes co-taught by Mentor Leaders rose dramatically.

As those of us who co-taught (or, at least, co-planned) worked together, the sense of community was heightened. Teaching and planning together only strengthened our reciprocal relationships. The mutual and dynamic interactions and exchanges of ideas and concerns that we have experienced required "a maturity that emerges from opportunities for meaning-making in sustainable communities" (Little 1982, 34).

We also realized that collaboration was an important part of the process for us and for our teacher candidates. If we modeled effective collaboration, then we were teaching our teacher candidates the value of that concept. If we openly reflected on our teaching and learning, we also modeled effective practices for them (Newby et al. 2000). These opportunities presented themselves in the planning and teaching arena within and without of our group.

> Collaborative planning along with co-teaching played a major role in my understanding of the content. Collaboration strengthened my teaching effectiveness by allowing me to see how other instructors teach. I must also say that it is imperative for a new member to also teach alone. This allows her to experiment with various teaching methods on her own. (LB)
>
> When colleagues share what they're doing in their respective classes and work together to make content and projects relative to one another, I think it's beneficial for students and for colleagues. (MG)
>
> This [collaborating] has been a fundamental means in helping me understand what each course may contain and how each may connect to others. It has been a slow evolution but I believe that we have a more solid grasp of the potential of our program. Much of this understanding has grown through informal conversations in meetings and in planning for courses. (DR)

As the Mentor Leader group grew and changed over time, there gradually emerged a new type of connectivity—one of looking at the meat of what we wanted our teacher candidates to take away with them. This began with conversations among members of the Mentor Leader group outside formal group meetings. As a result of those conversations, smaller groups emerged from within that were focused on specific issues in which they were interested.

> There are two sets of Mentor Leaders I really work with, the members of the book group and the other Secondary Mentor Leaders. Of the secondary folks, I work most closely with George because his office is so close to mine and we have similar goals for what we want for our students. (CA)
>
> I seem to have gravitated toward working mainly with the early childhood group of Mentor Leaders. I also work with the group writing this book, and our conversations have been very different from those that I have with my departmental colleagues. (VH)
>
> [I have affiliated with those who have an interest in] the relation of cognition and affect; the nature of intelligent behavior; how to nurture a deeper understanding of developmentally appropriate practice; promoting thoughtfulness about teaching and learning. (DR)
>
> I feel as if I have established professional relationships with many Mentor Leaders in a number of capacities. As I look to further my education I seek the advice and guidance of many Mentor Leaders. As I teach courses with a number of Mentor Leaders, I see my relationships growing in a professional manner. (LB)
>
> I find that the middle grades Mentor Leaders have a stronger bond (as I suspect is true with the early childhood Mentor Leaders). Since we deal with the same courses, requirements, issues, it is natural that we would be more likely to share and collaborate. (MG)

We began to see *reflective thinking* as an overarching idea for our program as a result of our being stimulated by two aspects of the program: one, by our deepened understanding of the importance of the laboratory setting for our teacher candidates as distinct from the demonstration school; and, two, by our awareness of the significance of collaboration to provoke new thinking from expanded perspectives.

This idea of reflective thinking was of significance to several members from early on. One of the Mentor Leaders had completed a dissertation on the relation between John Dewey's theory of imagination in reflective thinking and the practice of the teachers in the Chicago Laboratory School; another focused on the development of thinking in teacher candidates. The two often discussed the relative importance of affective and cognitive dimensions in the thinking process. Their continuing conversation led to an appreciation of Dewey's distinction between *rationality* and *reason.*

The whole Mentor Leader group was leavened by our examination of reflective thinking, in terms of our teacher candidates but also in terms of our own development as teacher educators. We talked about reflective thinking with one another and with our students, and we began formulating ideas about the importance of reflective thinking within our program. As our conversations continued, we discovered that *reflective thinking* had various definitions and that no one person thought reflectively in the same way. This diversity has added strength to the Mentor Leader group.

> I'm not sure that the ML conversations are responsible for my reflective thinking. Probably my one-on-one conversations with colleagues have played a greater role in this process. (MG)
>
> The one incident that I can recall challenging me to think reflectively would be dealing with a student who I felt didn't need to be in the program. Through many conversations with various Mentor Leaders at different times, I realized that I needed to reflect on what makes a teacher. I was in my second year when I noticed the change. (LB)
>
> I noticed a change in my thinking as I moved into my second year as a Mentor Leader. A smaller group of Mentor Leaders interested in concentrating on our craft emerged, and from our conversations and readings, the reflective thinking concept began to surface as an important part of our professional development. (VH)

A small group of faculty met to continue discussions about reflective thinking. At first, the discussions included quite a variety of department and school members, but as time went by, the locus of the group narrowed until the ones left were the authors of this book. As we continued discussing and exploring ways that we could continue to develop professionally, our conversations broadened, narrowed, and changed focus several times. Through many work sessions and discussions, we finally decided that our story could best be told by relating how the Mentor Leader group has developed over time and the direction that particular factions have taken. We wrote this material with the intent of informing our colleagues in the field of teacher preparation of our successes (and failures) as we established our Mentor Leader group.

Developing Professional Leadership: Mutual Affiliation to Shared Ideas

The shared purpose of the Mentor Leader group grew from conversations on common topics. From this sense of community, we began to notice that as the relationship deepened among members, a sense of caring emerged. As our relationship continued to evolve, our dialogue persisted and deepened. We talked about our relationships with teacher candidates, about what we wanted them to take with them as they left Georgia College & State University, and we realized that "As dialogue [among Mentor Leaders] unfolds, we participate in a mutual construction of the frame of reference . . . a sensitive task that involves total receptivity, reflection . . . and further exploration" (Noddings 1998, 191). We were doing just that! We had adopted an "ethic of care [which] requires us to recognize our frailty and to bring out the best in one another. It recognizes that we are dependent on each other" (191). This was evident in the ways we accepted, depended upon, encouraged, and challenged one another as we continued (and still continue) to grow in our profession.

> I see the ML group as offering me guidance in my role as a ML. If there are any questions that I may have I know that I can contact anyone in the ML group for advice. (LB)
> [The Mentor Leader group has become] a dynamic, diverse, provocative group committed to the hard work of continually

examining and improving our programs in teacher education. (DR)

Without the support of my peers I wouldn't have felt confident enough to fulfill tasks, nor would I have felt confident enough to step outside of my box and explore new roles for myself. (LB)

Embedded within the relationship of the members of our group is an element of trust. How do we project the element of trust to our members? Or do we? Is that the purpose of the group? Trust is an integral part of a reciprocal relationship. Reciprocity (Little 1982) means that we listen to one another; we give and receive feedback; and we learn from one another. These relationships require the capacity to care for oneself and for others, and to understand that our own growth and the growth of others are interconnected (Senge 1990). This implies trust within the group to speak freely without fear of admonition. Trust manifests itself in different ways through different people. From some of the comments we received, the issue of trust and the capacity to speak openly within the group are seen in a variety of ways.

> [I trusted the group] after my first complete year on the job. The feeling of trust emanates from the Mentor Leader group by the willingness of all members to help with any situation. No matter how "dumb" the new member may feel about having to ask some of their questions, not one Mentor Leader gives the impression that his time is being wasted. If anything, the members of the group go out of their way to help. (LB)
>
> I always feel free to speak openly. The times that I don't speak openly are those when I think my comments would be unnecessarily offensive to those who feel the need to hammer out minute details. (MG)
>
> There is a great diversity and range of opinion. I think that people listen to others and support reasonable discourse and permit disagreement. (DR)

Because of the element of trust that we established within the Mentor Leader group, we (at least most of us) feel comfortable challenging our colleagues to think deeply about their work with teacher candidates. Challenging our colleagues to explore the depth of their work is included in the "ethic of care" because caring includes coexploration. Coexploration reveals common interests and can help with understanding (Noddings 1998). If we initiate discussions with our colleagues on how we think about our work, then we are helping move our colleagues forward and are moving our relationships with our colleagues forward in a positive manner. We must be flexible thinkers when interacting with colleagues, listening and supporting them—not denigrating their thoughts, but encouraging them to think in different ways about their work. If we truly care about our colleagues, then "we accept the reality of . . . interdependence. Our goodness and our growth are inextricably bound to that of others we encounter" (Noddings 1998, 196).

Collaborating with colleagues publicly is one way to promote coexploration. Many entities are involved in the collaborative process of the Mentor Leader group. We deliberately interact with one another to revise and improve our program of teacher preparation so that our teacher candidates will be better prepared to enter the classroom. Interactions among group members influence issues such as changing the program of study, changing the focus of certain courses (typically to narrow the focus), and evaluating senior portfolios. All of these require flexibility, patience, understanding, and, again, the ability to show the "ethic of caring" when relating to another Mentor Leader.

> We work diligently with members from across campus to revise the material presented in content courses. This collaborative effort takes a monumental amount of flexibility and understanding in order to weave content, theory, and practice together in a meaningful way. (VH)
>
> Working with other Mentor Leaders and arts and sciences professors to develop content-rich courses that pay attention to social constructivist pedagogy requires more patience than you can imagine. Not everyone comes to the table with the same understanding of the needs of the course, and some come to the table with no understanding of the needs of the learner. But because we have a commitment to our students and the program, we work through any misunderstandings. It has been that way for the collaborative children's literature course. (LCH)

Professional Development:
Mutual Affiliation to Community

At times, a new Mentor Leader will have difficulty building a relationship with the group or any individuals. It is our responsibility to try to weave them into our group successfully. If we as a group can model the elements of the relationship that we see as important, we may be able to fold them into the group. It also denotes a further demonstration of caring, in that modeling shows "in our own behavior what it means to care [and therefore own our process and product of teacher education] . . . we do not merely tell them to care . . . we demonstrate our caring in our relations with them" (Noddings 1996, 190).

As we work with these new mentors, it may become clear that they are not interested in collaborating with the group for the greater gain. They may be interested only in the relationship itself without the ethic of professional development. They may not be interested in either the relationship or the professional responsibilities that come with the position. What do we do? Do we have an obligation to encourage them to remain with us? Would that be an honest response to what we believe? The responses we received from members of the group indicate that we have an obligation to support those members, to encourage them to become an active part of the group and an active participant in the work that we do.

> I think we do have an obligation to keep trying. When I first came, I was unclear about what the group really was and did, but as time passes I become more involved. (CA)
>
> I don't know that there is one particular thing that I could do on my own but I do feel that the ML group should work as a whole to encourage the new ML to remain with us. (LB)
>
> If there is a perception that program quality or integrity is compromised, then we do have an obligation to encourage collaboration. (MG)

At times a faculty member has come to the program, has not established any professional or personal relationships with members of the group, and has not willingly supported the school's mission. Even though members of the group have tried to work with that person, she or he has not responded in positive ways to our overtures. Typically, that faculty member opts out of the role.

It is clear that the Mentor Leader group has evolved from a loosely formed group that was struggling just to understand what to do next into a solidly formed group of faculty members who are dedicated to our common mission, preparing our teacher candidates to be effective classroom teachers when they leave our university.

We have found that although induction to the role is hard and sometimes frustrating, the experienced members do a fairly good job of orienting the new Mentor Leaders to their responsibilities. The job is very labor intensive, when you consider the time you must spend establishing relationships with principals and host teachers. Mentor Leaders spend a vast amount of time visiting the classrooms of their teacher candidates throughout the program. It is very rewarding to watch them grow and mature, both personally and professionally as they move from their junior year into the senior year.

Questions from the Book Authors

Campus: Main _____   Macon _____

How long have you been a member of the Mentor Leader group?

What was your educational background when you came to the Mentor Leader group?

How did the support you received from other Mentor Leaders to accomplish basic tasks lead you to become a member of the Mentor Leader group?

What are the important issues for inducting new members?

How has collaboration with your colleagues deepened your understanding of the content of the courses you teach and the ways in which you interact with your cohort teacher candidates—for example, reworking courses, collaborative planning, co-teaching?

How has collaboration with colleagues strengthened your teaching effectiveness?

How has collaboration with colleagues helped expose our teacher candidates to multiple perspectives?

How are your conversations with ML colleagues different now from your early conversations?

Do you feel comfortable within the ML group? Why? Why not?

When did you begin to have enough trust in the group to speak more freely about issues that concerned you?

Are there times when you don't feel free to speak openly? Why?

How does the feeling of trust emanate from the ML group? Or does it?

How have the conversations changed during ML meetings over time?

What is your perception of the Mentor Leader group at this point? Why?

How have conversations among Mentor Leaders challenged you to think reflectively (our favorite word!) about your work? Where were you in the induction process when you noticed a change?

Have you established professional relationships with particular MLs? If so, around what idea(s) is your relationship focused?

What has been your experience working as a team as you move through the junior ML experience into the senior ML experience? As you move through the MAT (master of arts of teaching) experience?

How do you help induct new Mentor Leaders into cohort-specific groups?

What do you do if a new ML is not responsive to collaborating with the group for the greater gain? Do you think we have an obligation to encourage that member to remain with us?

What do you do if a new ML is primarily interested in building a personal relationship but is not progressing toward embracing our professional ethic?

Program Specific to Music and HPER (Health, Physical Education, and Recreation)

How has being a member of the ML group affected you as a music ML or HPER ML?

Has your relationship with the group changed over time? How?

What issues relate across the programs?

How have you collaborated with members of the ML group from the School of Education (SOE)?

How has that collaboration influenced your thinking about your teaching and learning?

References

Lambert, L., M. Collay, M. Dietz, K. Kent, and A. Ershler Richert. 1996. *Who will save our schools? Teachers as constructivist leaders.* Thousand Oaks, CA: Corwin Press.

Little, J. W. 1982. Norms of collegiality and experimentations: Workplace conditions of school success. *AERA Journal* 19(3): 325–40.

Newby, T. J., D. A. Stepich, J. D. Lehman, and J. D. Russell. 2000. *Instructional technology for teaching and learning.* Upper Saddle River, NJ: Merrill.

Noddings, N. 1998. *Philosophy of education.* Boulder, CO: Westview Press.

Piaget, J. 1954. *The construction of reality in the child.* Translated by M. Cook. New York: Basic Books.

Rosenholtz, S. J. 1991. *Teachers' workplace: The social organization of schools.* New York: Teachers College Press.

Senge, P. M. 1990. *The fifth discipline: The art and practice of the learning organization.* New York: Doubleday.

Vygotsky, L. 1962. *Thought and language.* Boston: MIT Press.

Vygotsky, L. 1978. *Mind in society.* Cambridge, MA: Harvard University Press.

3

A Conversation on Integrating Theory and Practice

Cynthia J. Alby

> . . . ideas about learning [should start] in real problems
> encountered by student teaching during field experi-
> ences. The student teacher would then develop his or
> her own knowledge in a process of reflection on the
> practical situations in which a personal need for learn-
> ing we created.
>
> —Korthagen and Kessels, Linking Theory and
> Practice: Changing the Pedagogy of Teacher
> Education, *Educational Researcher, 28*(4), 7

> *Much of our collaborative work develops in the conversations we
> have with other Mentor Leaders. Chapter 2 considers the prem-
> ises under which we choose to collaborate. Chapter 3 is a virtual
> conversation, modeling a typical generative conversation.*

CYNTHIA: Vicki, I've been thinking that it would be a great idea
to write this chapter in the form of a conversation. I mean, dialogue is at the heart of our professional community here, and
people might like to see what that dialogue looks like. I can still
cover the topic of how we integrate theory and practice, but in a
different format.

VICKI: I think that is a great idea. Let's try it out.

CYNTHIA: I've got my basic questions and a tape recorder, so
we'll see what happens. Know what else might be good? I could

go back later and add in some of the theorists who have especially influenced us. Put them in like they were literally part of the conversation. That would be something, a real tribute to dialogue!

PAULO FREIRE: I love this idea, Cynthia. In dialogue, "the object to be known is put on the table *between* the subjects of knowing. They meet around it and through it for mutual inquiry" (Shor and Freire 1987, 99).

CYNTHIA: How do you think teaching experiences can guide theory development?

NANCY: Do you mean the teaching we do with the candidates or the teaching they do in the schools?

CYNTHIA: I think I mean teacher candidates' experiences in the classroom. Well, not just their public school teaching experiences, but their observations there, too.

LEIGH: Well, yes and no. As soon as you say "teaching experiences," I think about all kinds of reflective practice.

CYNTHIA: So we mean when candidates watch us teach, when they watch their host teacher teach, when they reflect on their own teaching—all three of those. Oh, and their past experiences as students themselves.

LEIGH: Even their concurrent courses with other faculty who lecture more or whatever. Whatever instructional strategy the professor chooses to use becomes a vehicle for discussion.

VICKI: True.

LEIGH: If it's more along the lines of metatheory, strands that guide their own theory, then it gives them a vehicle to identify, or give a voice to, what they think teaching and learning are. And while that is by no means capital "T" theory, it gives them a moment to make a claim. And by having that level of agency to make claims about what they believe teaching and learning to be, it gives them a level of confidence. I think they are more likely to consider the power of the teacher if we make the spaces to make those claims.

DEE: I would say, practice and theory can't exist without one another. We're always generalizing based on previous experience. That's what a theory is. As human beings, whenever we enter a new situation we're always bringing with us all that prior experience. The question is, are we going to be conscious of what we bring to the situation, or are we going to be acting on an impulse based on our prior knowledge? If we're able to be reflective, have some sense about the ideas we're using to interpret a situation, then we can perhaps make better decisions. This outlook is stated by Dr. Dewey, particularly in "How We Think."

CYNTHIA: It's asking a lot of some students to think like that.

DEE: It's asking a lot of *all* people. It's asking a lot of some faculty members. [Laughter]

KARYNNE: I guess it was in my struggles of not communicating well with other teachers when I was a middle school teacher that I realized you need a coherent theory, and you need to be able to articulate it. You will save yourself much grief. I'm not sure if you can tell a person that. But if you just go into a school and start teaching, you will run into problems, and you won't even know what the problem *is*. That's because you don't know theory. You don't realize that the students are acting out of this and you're acting out of that. Our role is to challenge some of the perspectives they come with, the typical way of looking at a situation. Like, "The teacher is doing that to be nice." No, maybe the teacher is being coercive or buying time.

VICKI: And you've got to have those teaching experiences in order to help the students understand how the theory is applicable.

They can read about it, and we can talk about it, but to me it's like anything else; I learn better by application. We've got to give them the opportunity to go into their placements and apply what they've learned or experiment with it—try out some of the methods that different theorists suggest. Then when they write about what happened, it causes them to process what they've done.

CYNTHIA: Right.

VICKI: That's what happened to me in college. I learned about the theorists, but then that was gone, and several semesters later I went into student teaching. No one ever said a word about theory. There was no connection at all between the theoretical and what happened in my student teaching. Research suggests that unless you have certain types of instruction, you teach as you were taught, and that is exactly what I did.

DEBORAH BRITZMAN: "From the start, teacher education was conceived of as synonymous with vocational preparation" (1991, 29). "I propose a dialogic restructuring of teacher education that begins with the recognition that multiple realities, voices, and discourses conjoin and clash in the process of coming to know" (1991, 33).

CYNTHIA: And we have the perfect venue for doing that because our candidates are in the schools at the same time they are taking classes, in the case of the undergraduates, for two years. So there is a lot of time to process, conjoin, and clash. And I think so much of what we require of our candidates is specifically designed to help them recognize multiple realities, voices, and discourses.

SONYA NIETO: Lilia Bartolome (1994) has criticized what she calls "the methods fetish" in most teacher preparation programs and schools. . . . She asserts that "the teacher's politically clear educational philosophy" (179) is far more important than specific methods (1999, 80).

CYNTHIA: What are some specific experiences you've designed for your students to help them see the relationship between theory and practice?

KARYNNE: One thing I like to do is have candidates identify critical incidents that would help them develop a cohesive framework and then that framework becomes the theory.

LEIGH: What do you mean by "helping them to identify critical incidents"?

KARYNNE: I just say, think about things that made an impression on you, good or bad. Like even when they do the writing samples at the very beginning when they talk about a favorite teacher or a negative experience in school. I ask, "Why did you pick *that* one? Why does that stick out?" You need someone with more experience to help you identify why you really picked that incident. I look at what I think is an underlying message. I look for a pattern: "The teacher always listened to everyone. . . . The teacher didn't play favorites. . . . The teacher expected me to do my best. . . . Some people thought she was mean but I thought she was great." "What in you was resonating that made you think she was great but others thought she was mean?" "Well, I could tell she had an expectation of me." I try to get at the underlying message, "Oh, so a teacher should be a motivator? Should the teacher be the same for all the children, motivate the same way for everyone?" It's my theory about their theory, and I'm never certain that I'm accurate; but I think I have enough experience that I usually am accurate.

VICKI: One of the things I've done right at the beginning of first semester in their learning theory class is journaling. We talk about the theorists, and we also talk about the experiences they are having in their classrooms. How does what they see fit in with what we are studying? We come up with questions together, and we decide what they will look for. Observe your teacher, write about what she is doing, the way she is teaching, and then see if you can take that and put it into Piaget or Vygotsky or whomever we happen to be discussing.

DEE: Yes. Definitely the first thing is to help students develop the ability to observe children carefully and start to see the patterns either in individual children or across a number of children. That looking for patterns based on good, clear observation is the beginning of generating theory. It helps ground our students in observation. It is also important that our candidates examine theoretical statements made by other people and begin to try to see how those help them make sense of what they are observing. There is a give-and-take between the situation and the understandings you bring to make sense of them.

VICKI: Tell me more about that.

DEE: Well, one of the techniques I've used, especially initially, is to keep a kind of ethnographic journal based on note *taking* and note *making*. On one side of the page, *take* notes. The notes should be as descriptive as possible, and then the note making is to help them understand that their generalizations are note *making*. And if they can begin to separate those so that first they can become good anecdotal record takers, then they may be able to use those notes to look for patterns.

LEIGH: If what we're attempting to do is to inculcate somebody who is willing to be a reflective practitioner, then one of the things we are focusing on is having the teacher candidates deconstruct their teaching experiences to get at the deeper levels of critical thinking and inquiry and trying to figure out, "Okay, now that I've looked at this example of my own teaching . . . " Or our own teaching. One thing I do with my own classes is to say, "During class I used this particular technique. Why? What is going on with that? What did it do for you as a learner? Why would I choose to do this as a teacher? What do you think I hoped to get, and what did I actually get?"

CYNTHIA: When I think about this past year, it was harder for me to help my students see the relationship between theory and practice because, due to state pressures, I was forced to start the program in the summer. So they were not concurrently in classrooms. Then how do you make it work? I had to rely more on drawing upon their past experiences and helping them link those to the theorists we were studying. And also I modeled different things myself. Then at the end of class I would stop and say, "This is what I did. Why do you think I did it?" We dissected my practice. I found they were willing to give the theories more of a fair shake because they were looking at them in terms of what had or had not worked for them, as learners instead of looking through the eyes of a teacher.

NANCY: I am more likely to come in at the beginning of class and reflect on what happened the last time and why I have struggled in between. But as far as the kind of assignments I have designed for them, I like to have them try out something in class with their peers and then talk about what has happened along with linking that with theory. Then they take those ideas and design something they are going to try out in their field placements and in turn reflect on those experiences.

CYNTHIA: So when we talk about teaching experiences, we should broaden the concept even further to include our candidates teaching their peers.

NANCY: Now that my seniors are in the field all day, I've created a website so they can continue to share and reflect. It has been interesting to see the ones who have been posting and the ones who have not. The ones who have, I have seen changes in their ideas. I can see them being able to bring their ideas together. Those who are not interacting and not verbalizing are more lost.

LEIGH: For the middle grades group, I have them do miscue analysis. They see something going on with a reader, and they have to figure out, what can I do for this child? And so I have them go through the steps of paying attention to learners and paying attention to what learners are doing. Being deliberate in the analysis of how the learner is exhibiting certain things. And then coming back and saying, "What does that mean for teaching? What do I need to do now?" It helps to them to position themselves as a teacher and an assessor.

CYNTHIA: Yeah. I can remember you telling me about the tapes you made where you were trying hard to make miscues for your students to analyze.

LEIGH: In general, I tend towards activities that are focused, connected to P–12 students, and where our candidates are required to make decisions about the information they are gathering and support those with theory.

DEE: Another assignment that we do in the integrated culture and language class is to have them go through a neighborhood, draw a map of the neighborhood, and offer a descriptive account of that neighborhood. We deliberately look at the assumptions they are making and challenge them to think of alternative ways to interpret that. We want them to become conscious of the ways they are already making generalizations based on prior experiences that may or may not be accurate. Then we ask them to find evidence that might support one interpretation or another. Those kinds of themes carry throughout all kinds of assignments. When they are writing anything, we ask them to support whatever they claim with good, clear evidence, repeatedly going back to whatever they are working on to root it in good observations.

NANCY: One of the ideas I really want my students to understand is integrated instruction and what that really means. Building on Beane's idea of what integrated instruction is, last spring I tried consciously to model the entire semester after his theory so the students could experience that as a learner. I did that because almost nowhere in the state could I take them to a classroom and see this theory in action. Furthermore, my candidates became very involved in designing their own curriculum.

CYNTHIA: I haven't found many great videos that illustrate specific teaching practices. Maybe we could arrange with a host teacher to really prepare a lesson that will illustrate a practice in a clear way, and we could videotape it and use it for years to come.

NANCY: I'd love to use some of our own graduates.

LEIGH: What about classroom research? Even if they never write it up as a formal paper, it can be a great way to link theory and practice.

KARYNNE: When I meet with students individually or I'm responding to journals, I am trying to say, "This is what I think your theory is, what do you think your theory is? And why is it important to have a theory? Why does a person with one theory act this way and a person with another theory act another way?" I think all my private interactions with students are really about that in one way or another, probably some of my classroom interactions, too. I'm gathering data all the time, but I'm not always putting it out there in such a way that I'm asking them to examine it.

CYNTHIA: It sounds like at first you do a lot of the work for them. Do they reach a point where they ask your questions of themselves?

KARYNNE: They do reach a point where they recognize that they have a theory and everyone has a theory. They start seeing differences in people. I won't say they all reach it. With some of them I keep saying, "Take another look; take another look."

CYNTHIA: What other types of activities have you all designed?

KARYNNE: Well, we've been talking about activities, but for me it is really less about activities and more about a way of being. I myself continually model what I hope they will do themselves. I might say, "I was thinking this and then I did that, and I recognized I really do think this way about, say, time. Maybe that's a problem. Maybe I need to think some more about that. How is this affecting my class when I am always worrying about time?" Another reason I think of it as a way of being is that I frequently commend teachers for their intellect and teachers who are intellectual about their profession. I hold that up in very high esteem, and I think my candidates get the message that "That is what I should be doing. It isn't enough to just go through the motions, I need to know why I am going through the motions." I think they realize that that is important to me, and they think that is a good thing. They want to be like that.

NANCY: So you require a lot of reflection.

KARYNNE: Yes, and I'm doing it aloud.

NANCY: Is it more likely to be verbal than written?

KARYNNE: I'm more likely to see how they are thinking when it is written, but I do more of the guiding verbally.

DEE: Do you play devil's advocate or turn questions back to them?

KARYNNE: I don't think I play devil's advocate. I say, "I know I could be totally wrong about this, but this is what I see." So I try to lay the groundwork that mine is just one opinion, hopefully one you're valuing. If you think I'm wrong, here is your chance to tell me what you really think is going on here. For example, I might say, "I do think your middle class upbringing has an effect on what you're doing." Or, "I do think you're thinking of your middle school experience as the only valid middle school experience." And I'll just lay it out there. If I'm wrong, you need to help me see. Usually it gets some good discussion going. I usually think I *am* right! [Everyone laughs.] I rarely have someone say, "No, that is way off base."

CYNTHIA: **What texts do you use?**

KARYNNE: Any? [Laughter] I do have my candidates read some theory, but I'm less insistent that they necessarily read it and more insistent that they are conversant in it. They do read Dewey's *How We Think*, which is pretty involved for undergraduates. I don't have them read Vygotsky because I can't think of any one part that I think says it all, but I expect them to know the principles from Vygotsky that I base my practice on. Bruner, James, Duckworth . . . Some think it is good to be eclectic. I do not think it is good to be eclectic. They may say they take a little from here and a little from there, but the theories are in opposition.

VICKI: I still like Woolfolk's *Educational Psychology.* I like that book because it is a good reference book to have.

CYNTHIA: Is it more actual excerpts from the theorists or summaries and interpretations?

VICKI: It is more of an interpretation.

CYNTHIA: So you have your students doing less of reading the theorists themselves and more of reading the theory.

VICKI: Right, and that I want to change. I want them to read pieces from the actual theorists. I saw Leigh's list of readings, and I liked a lot of what she had on it. I'm probably going to use Piaget, Dewey, Vygotsky, and some behavioristic stuff. They need to know a little Skinner and then some Bandura. Then of course I also want to focus on the cognitive, the brain research. And I want to get them involved right away with multiple intelligences.

CYNTHIA: I think we are starting to see Gardner as one of the major theorists.

DEE: Dewey is very important to me, but I have not had them read Dewey in a number of years. In the past I had them read *School and Society,* but he is very difficult in some ways. Particularly in early childhood, a theorist who is very important for us to consider is Piaget. We look at his work in one of the first classes they take. As Vicki said, another theorist who is important to us is Howard Gardner and the notion of multiple intelligences. I have a desire, too, to have our candidates become familiar with some of our past, great forerunners, and particularly women. So from time to time I have used such books as *Teacher* by Sylvia Ashton Warner, who really is able to recount her experiences in light of her own theoretical understanding. I think that is a good book for our students because of her passion and commitment. I also will make sure they know the work of Susan Issacs, who was British, active in the 1920s. She was a very careful anecdotal record taker, looking at theoretical application, Freudian and Piagetian.

LEIGH: Developmental learning theory tends to come out of an essentialized text, third person, a tertiary text. It tends to center around cognitivism, social constructivism, information processing system, and with a healthy dose of behaviorism, so Kohlberg and Erikson. Of course some Piaget and Vygotsky. I tend to throw in Wersch. But I also have them look at primary research articles in classroom research while they are looking at the broader theory to get the basic understanding.

CYNTHIA: That makes sense.

LEIGH: We did an experiment with the early childhood children's literature class of having them read primary texts, and that was really challenging. Bettleheim is a challenge! A couple groups read it, and they did have enough savvy to determine if it had relevance. I'm becoming more and more sold on bringing in more primary texts and letting them muck around with the heavy stuff.

NANCY: I've done some stuff with Dewey and Beane. And depending what topic they chose, they had to find primary sources to go along with that. For example, different theories of motivation, comparing and contrasting things like intrinsic and extrinsic motivation theory. They've also done primary reading in ethics and law, cases and so forth.

CYNTHIA: Now that we're talking about this, there are some relatively modern theorists who I would like my students to read. Brooks is very accessible to students, and Fosnot is good too. I like to add a bit of Bruner too.

CYNTHIA: **What do students especially struggle with?**

VICKI: It takes them a whole semester before they can focus on what's really important. At first, they tend to want to focus on the physical things the teacher does. They want to focus on the schedule, the seating arrangements. They have to make the transition from "The teacher got up in front of the class and taught addition," to how she taught addition and what techniques she used. Do those techniques fit with theorist A or theorist B? I think it is actually making the transition from looking at the classroom as just a schedule of events to looking within the actual method. They have to analyze and dissect and name it.

LEIGH: For me, they latch on to the language pretty quickly. A functional use of the concepts, they struggle with.

NANCY: They can talk it, and they can even tell you what ought to be happening. They will say things like, they know that their classroom ought to be student-centered, but they still don't have a handle on what that means.

LEIGH: Making the claims is easy; doing it is hard. And they don't necessarily have examples of the things we are talking about.

DEE: The most difficult thing is to start questioning your own assumptions. In some ways, to read a theory, to know about it, to be able to talk about it, can be fairly easy. But to then start really applying it . . . It is difficult to really even *see* the situation. I'm getting ready to say something right from Dewey's *Art and Experience*. It is so easy to label a situation, "Oh, this child is such and such," instead of taking the time to look carefully, to receive, to almost enter passively into trying to understand and receive that child.

CYNTHIA: Karynne, I really hope that you do go back to a middle school classroom to get your National Board certification, because I would love to bring a few of my students to your class from time to time, and we could videotape you. If fact, in a year or two, I hope to do National Board myself. I would invite my candidates to come in and see what I am doing. Then they couldn't say anymore that certain methods aren't possible.

LEIGH: They have a hard time recognizing how much of what goes on in a classroom is teacher's choice and teacher's power, that what they choose to do and not do impacts learning. I wonder if our candidates have the mental image of the principal walking in, taking the pencil out of their hand, and saying, "Leave the room! I won't let you do this anymore!"

NANCY: My students like to say that when they have their own classroom, it will be different. And I'm thinking, "I'm afraid it's not. If you can't show me in your student teaching what you can do, don't try to convince me that when it's your own classroom you'll be able to make it different."

LEIGH: I am concerned about that passivity. "The host teacher doesn't want me to . . . " I can remember my host teacher giving me suggestions, and then I would do what I wanted to. It was my student teaching and my time to teach. Our candidates sometimes take a suggestion as a mandate. We may need to work with our host teachers on that.

NANCY: I think that the host teachers I am working with are more open than the candidates want to admit. Sometimes the candidates use it as a crutch.

CYNTHIA: I have a candidate with the most controlling host teacher ever, and she manages to subvert this all the time.

CYNTHIA: What do you do to support your students as they initially struggle to connect theory and practice?

VICKI: We talk a lot in class. They talk. Sometimes I talk too much. I try to catch myself and turn it back to then. But the main thing is providing the venue for discussion and trying to get them to the point where they value the professional discussions.

So I think the main thing I do first is build community. If we can do that, then that provides a more risk-free environment. When they first start, conversation is tentative. But now that I have them in their senior year, I can't shut them up!

CYNTHIA: How do I give that support? One thing that I do is I try to be really careful about giving my opinion because they will say, "You know the answer; which of these theories is the best theory?" Part of me does want to say, "This one is!"

LISA DELPIT: The teacher cannot be the only expert in the classroom. To deny students their own expert knowledge *is* to disempower them (1995, 32).

CYNTHIA: Well, in reality I know that a lot depends on who your students are and what your local situation is. I want my students to recognize that all that has to be taken into consideration. So another way I support them later is by having them do an assessment of a class and the class environment and require that they use that as they talk about which methods and theories best apply to that specific situation.

LISA DELPIT: I threw out all the desks and added carpeted open learning areas. I was doing what I learned, and it worked. Well, at least it worked for some of the children. My white students zoomed ahead. My black students . . . practiced karate moves on the new carpets. Some of them even learned to read, but none of them as quickly as the white students (1995, 13).

VICKI: I like what you and Lisa had to say about empowering students to share their own knowledge. Do you find you have to build community before students will readily share their opinions?

CYNTHIA: Absolutely. Students have to be comfortable before they will share their opinions. One thing I do is utilize "opinionnaires." Those are questionnaires that really are just looking for your opinion. I want them to get down on paper where they stand on what we are about to discuss. That way, students are more likely to say they disagree because they have it on paper. They are clear on where they stand because they thought about it beforehand. And if they are going to change their minds, research shows that it is important that their preconceptions are visible to them first. If you ignore the preconceptions, students are more likely to revert to the preconceptions later.

JOHN BRANSFORD: Students come to the classroom with preconceptions about how the world works. If their initial understanding is not engaged, they may fail to grasp the new concepts and information that are taught, or they may learn them for purposes of a test but revert to their preconceptions outside of class (1999, 10).

LEIGH: Part of it comes in the developmental theory class where candidates from early childhood and middle grades are mixed in one integrated studies class. Quite often the conversations that happen are deconstructing what is going on in their science class in order for them to understand, "what are we doing in identification groups?" Because the learning that takes place in that science class does not make them comfortable. Potentially the scaffolding we provide is to help them take the initial step of analyzing what is uncomfortable about it and what is the potential for that discomfort to increase their learning.

CYNTHIA: What about it makes them so uncomfortable?

LEIGH: A variety of things. Being placed inside of identification groups, having three or four instructors, the types of activities they do. They say, "We aren't being lectured at; this must not be science." There is not a single textbook. There is a whole range of things that are essentially socially constructed learning, and they are not used to it.

NANCY: Plus the learning logs and the levels of reflection that they are expected to accomplish and the way that's set up for them to have to apply theory. They are uncomfortable with that.

So we help them by requiring that they be explicit, and we ask them specific questions to help them do that. "What exactly does that mean, what you have just written in your learning log?"

CYNTHIA: How would you describe that learning log?

LEIGH: It is something they do in the science class where there are three levels of reflection that can be evidenced—technical, which would be a technical level with no evaluation whatsoever. Then there is a contextual where you start noting the contextual variables, which are connected to that level of summary. Then you have dialectical, which looks at the implications. "If I am a teacher in a classroom and I make a decision about teaching ecology in this oil-based industry town, what does that mean for the students and what the community sees?" So it is going beyond into the social and political aspects of what we do and why we do it.

LEIGH: I think most of the scaffolding we do is more towards identifying themselves as teachers and learners. When they first come, they make tons of claims about what is good teaching. "How do you know? I know it when I see it." They say they are in teaching because they love children and they want to help. There is almost nothing critical in those initial stages. And I think that the scaffolding comes in continually holding the mirror up to them, but then helping them talk about what they are seeing, giving them a language to use for what they think they see in that teacher in that mirror. They don't always like what they see especially when they learn about certain practices and how they potentially don't support learners unless they are used in very particular ways. What they thought was good teaching and worked for them doesn't work for 90 percent of the population. And part of the scaffolding is the group building and the support we give one another so we can also be critical of each other. That includes the Mentor Leaders. We're allowed to say, "You know, I didn't do that really well. And I can tell it wasn't going well because of these things."

NANCY: And another big part of it is helping them see things from different perspectives: from the perspective of the students, the host teacher, the administration. "If you were the adminis-trator for this school, how would you be thinking of this?" A lot of what we do is to try to ask the right questions to make this happen.

FRED KORTHAGEN: I can really appreciate your ideas about how theory and teaching experiences come together. Why? Because ideas about learning should "take their starting point in real problems encountered by student teachers during field experi-ences. The student teacher would then develop his or her own knowledge in a process of reflection on the practical situations in which a personal need for learning was created" (Korthagen & Kessels 1999, 7). I can see how that is just what you are doing.

CYNTHIA: How have your views on the importance of using prac-tice to develop theory changed because of the collaboration with your colleagues here?

VICKI: When I first came here I would have used different words to describe what I know to be effective. This group has taught me a better vocabulary for putting these ideas into words. I re-ally enjoy these types of conversations, like we're having now.

CYNTHIA: I've seen the value of having both the theoretical and practical together.

VICKI: Yes, we need people who tend to be more philosophical as well as those of us who are more grounded in the practical. My big picture I had when I came here is now a lot bigger.

CYNTHIA: I think of all the Mentor Leaders; you and I are most similar in that. We have a philosophical side, but the practical is of such great importance to us. We're so interested in the practical nitty-gritty of the classroom. In fact, I would say that one of the primary reasons I came into this position is that I was starting to lose that balance. I didn't have that ongoing professional discussion because I was a department of one at my previous job. That is when I started hanging out here with you all.

CYNTHIA: The parallels between what we do as a professional community and what we encourage our students to do fascinate me. It wasn't that obvious to me before I asked you all these specific questions. Look at us talking about how our vocabulary has changed as a result of working together and what that change brings to how we talk about things and how we understand things. And then look at how several of you mentioned the importance of introducing your students to a vocabulary and how that advances their discussions of theory and practice, and changes the very way they think about those things.

KARYNNE: I'm more tolerant of people who are at different places than I am. I still try to move them to other places but . . . And I'm more comfortable with what *I know.* That has come because of collaboration. I don't necessarily agree with all the approaches of everyone in the group, but I'm less anxious to change them. I've also learned that a softer approach will generally be a better approach. Now it may not look to an outside person like I have a softer approach, [laughter] but I actually do!

CYNTHIA: Don't you think that is something we do with our students when we help them build community? We try to help them feel more tolerant of others' ideas even if they don't necessarily agree with them. Plus you talked about how you have become more comfortable with what you know. That certainly happens with our candidates. When I attend the Senior Showcase and talk to the candidates about the research they have done, they are so confident. They've talked so much with their peers about their own ideas that they're ready to talk to anyone who walks up.

NANCY: Leigh and Karynne have affected how the Mentor Leader group looks at theory and practice. I see that it is much more important than I thought when I came here. I didn't put it in words when I came here. I did it—some, but I tended to put more emphasis on practice. I didn't have students talking about the theory I was asking them to implement. So it's been a huge transformation for me to be associated with this group. And then Cynthia joined the group. I just sit back in awe and think, "These people are so smart and know so much, and I don't know any of this stuff." A lot of what is going into this book is a learning process for me. When you ask me these questions you are asking, I really have to stop and think. And I'm still struggling with the issue of what the theory is that undergirds what I think of as effective practice. I'm still working on it.

CYNTHIA: I hope your students can see how you model theory development as an ongoing process.

LEIGH: I came in with the troubling question of theory and practice, having just read books like *Practice Makes Practice*. I saw candidates coming out of programs with vast, year-long experiences, and they weren't necessarily any better than students coming out of traditional programs. They were more adept at school culture, but they weren't necessarily better teachers. I saw some pretty terrible teaching practices replicated because there was that extensive exposure, and they didn't have that critique, that reflection. You aren't practicing atheoretically. Everything you do is based on something even if it is a best guess because you can't articulate it. I found a location of people with whom I could figure out what I think I know. And I could have people like Karynne and Dee challenge me. Too often, people don't challenge me. If you can talk a lot and talk a good game . . .

CYNTHIA: And use big words!

LEIGH: Yes, and use big words, people won't challenge you. So I found people who would. To not only say it but to do it and think about how it gets done. Every year I've taught developmental learning theory I've taught it differently and used a different book. I've kept a few of the core activities but refined them. And some that didn't seem to have an effect or didn't have the effect I wanted, I radically revamped in various ways. That would not necessarily happen without other people with whom to have conversations, who have new ideas, who read other things and say, "I just read . . . did you know . . . "

CYNTHIA: I can imagine readers reading what you just said and saying, "Well, I can't do this because the people I work with aren't interested in this themselves.

LEIGH: At any one school you can find one other person. You may not find them until a year down the road, but you do find someone who is interested in reading and discussing and talking even if it is a pair at first. I think it is because I've chosen to pursue it that I've found it everywhere I have worked. And if you literally have one hundred colleagues and literally not one wants to sit and talk, then I'm not sure you should be there.

NANCY: We are, what? Six people? We're early childhood and middle grades and secondary. You can find people.

DEE: What has changed is my own practice, my own ability to be specific in what I look for and what I question, my ability to become more dogged. Some of it has to do with some of the questioning my colleagues undertake with me. Certainly Karynne, who has been here longest, because of her emphasis on rationality, would elicit a lot of questions and comments from me, and she would return that. Early on we undertook an examination of reflective thinking. It is the doggedness of all of you, that persistent self-examination and questioning.

CYNTHIA: See, there it is again. We're trying to get our candidates to see self-examination as second nature because that has worked so well for us. Do you see what I keep saying? Consciously and unconsciously we've tried to create professional communities in our cohorts that mirror what has worked for us as a professional community. To some degree we knew we were doing that, but now as I think back on all we've said here today, I see that we've re-created our successes in minute detail in some cases. And this is just one example. Today we were just talking about the integration of theory and practice; I'll bet we'd see even more interesting parallels between the professional community we've created and the ones we attempt to help our cohorts build if we looked at a different topic.

VICKI: Girl, have you looked at your watch lately? Let's save that for one of those many days where we are all just sitting around doing nothing.

CYNTHIA: Like after we retire?

VICKI: Yeah, that will be our next book.

References

Bartolome, L. I. 1994. Beyond the methods fetish: Toward a humanizing pedagogy. *Harvard Educational Review* 64: 173–94.

Britzman, D. 1991. *Practice makes practice.* New York: State University of New York Press.

Delpit, L. 1995. *Other people's children.* New York: The New Press.

Donovan, M. S., J. D. Bransford, and J. W. Pellegrino, eds. 1999. *How people learn: Bridging research and practice.* New York: National Academy Press.

Korthagen, F. A., and J. P. A. M. Kessels. 1999. Linking theory and practice: Changing the pedagogy of teacher education. *Educational Researcher* 28(4): 4–17.

Nieto, S. 1999. *The light in their eyes.* New York: Teachers College Press.

Shor, I., and P. Freire. 1987. A pedagogy of liberation: Dialogues on transforming education. New York: Bergin & Garvey.

4

Promoting Integration of Learning through Inquiry

Leigh Craft Hern

> The school must meet the unique needs and interests of the child, while providing a situation where the problem-solving processes used by both children and adults can be brought to bear upon those interests and those needs.
>
> —Mayhew and Edwards, *Dewey School*, (1936/1966, 250)

From our conversations (chapter 3), we integrate our theories into our Mentor Leader meetings and teaching practices, modeling inquiry for our cohort students.

Any professional program of study will require specific assignments to promote the goals of the program. In ours we have designed assignments specifically to engender positive change in our teacher candidates on the dimensions of reflectivity, collaboration, and commitment to teaching and learning. The purposeful engagement required by assignments coupled with Mentor Leader support assists them in developing from unreflective thinkers to reflective practitioners with a positive disposition toward inquiry (Kleine 2000). Despite our candidates' initial low levels of reflective practice (technical rationality; see Schön 1987, 1991), routine formal assessment of their development reveals consistent progression toward the highest levels of reflection. Candidates' sophisticated articulation of their teaching theories, identities, and practices are indicative of our success in achieving programmatic intent—to produce Architects of Change.

We are in part successful on these three fronts because in continual discourse we ask our teacher candidates to provide rationales for their actions, evidence for their claims. We are far less interested in helping them espouse a particular position as we are in having them determine a position and ascertaining why they are committed to that position. In journals, through work samples, and in class discussions we frequently ask, "How did you arrive at that conclusion? On what are you basing this claim? Have you considered that from another position?" This strategy has the effect of advancing their intellects and cultivating a disposition of judiciousness while provoking their desire to engage in ongoing inquiry. Again, this professional practice of asking for substantiation of statements and subjecting thoughts to deep scrutiny is one modeled and expected in the Mentor Leader group as a method for resolving disequilibrium and refining teaching theory. New members are socialized to this expectation for being experimenters in education.

Modeling Integrative Practices

The administration of a teaching university traditionally expects teaching excellence from its faculty, yet that expectation does not presume integrative or reflective practices. At Georgia College & State University, connected to our initial preparation programs, a pattern of integrative practices has developed through the Mentor Leader group. Academics hired to fulfill Mentor Leader duties are invited to attend meetings where more experienced Mentor Leaders offer their patterns of conduct to the new member. Some of those patterns integrate problems encountered, avenues of resolution, and consideration for effectiveness. In addition to such offerings, discussions of integrative practices are the daily business of the meetings. Mentor Leaders often send topics and events for discussion, which become the agenda for the meetings. Most of these topics are problem-based—for example, working with a school principal who is resistant to the classroom assignments our teacher candidates carry out in P–12 settings, or negotiating how standards designed for the whole school are met by all programs. In Mentor Leader meetings, we examine everything from class scheduling and P–12 placements to course rigor. Other group members help to generate solutions that will uphold the standards of the program while attending to the contextual complexities that make the problem unique. The individual Mentor Leader then selects an action—whether derived from the advice of the group or from her or his own informed experience—and then evaluates the effectiveness of the solution. We identify this process as "integrative practice" when a deliberate code of conduct—a process supporting reflective practice—is used.

We define integrative practice within Schön's reflective practitioner model (1983, 1987, 1991), where an "expert" brings all knowledge, skills, and dispositions to bear to solve unique problems. Professions that are historically defined as applied sciences (nursing, teaching, drafting, landscaping, etc.) are often perceived as "technical." Some researchers imply that those professions are technical because they believe that the problems that "technical practitioners" face are well-structured and unidimensional. Solutions can be and are predetermined based on a variety of behavioral or cognitive learning theories. Should a particular problem persist, then the "technician" would conclude that the problem is misidentified or perhaps the wrong solution was identified.

Technicians tend to view practice through a reductionist's lens. Problems encountered are simplified; solutions are selected and applied. Solutions are often generated from unexamined theories. Technicians consult solutions offered by a range of "how-to" resources—which (for teachers) may be how to use prewriting strategies, to start the school year right, to create an effective learning environment, and so forth—and they apply the solution they felt "might work." Should the solution fail, the technicians may decide that they had misidentified the problem or had selected the wrong solution. For a technician, there is always an appropriate answer for any given predicament.

Public school teachers have long been considered technicians, rather than professionals, and have been "trained" as
such. If the teacher would just follow the teacher's manual and
consistently apply the school rules, then children would learn,
and there would be few or no management problems. While few
people, even those least informed of schooling, still believe that
teaching is this simplistic, there is the "feel" that teaching retains
many technical features and that decisions do not hinge upon informed reflection. Rather than rely on the decisions of informed,
reflective practitioners, school boards and county curriculum of-
fices rely on textbooks and teaching kits, and they demand that
teachers implement the packaged, deskilled, standard programs.
It takes time to become adept at the inquiry process necessary
for reflective practice—time which, all too often, school board
leaders do not value or support.

For the Mentor Leader group, much time in becoming a reflective practitioner centers on the academic developing a strong understanding of "I" (Whitehead 2000). A reflective practitioner
cannot respond to the question of "how can I improve my practice?" if she or he does not understand how "I" operates among the
variables of teaching. A Mentor Leader cannot become a reflective
practitioner—a person who can consciously consider the "ethical
implications and consequences of teaching practice" (Larrivee
2000, 293)—without understanding the "I." Examination of the "I"
brings explanations of professional learning under the light. Practitioners develop their education theories as they relate to the development of their students. A philosophy of education becomes a
lived experience, rather than a created document, because a practitioner is challenged daily to observe the effects of his or her
choices. Mentor Leaders infuse personal beliefs and values into a
professional identity and employ a deliberate code of conduct. Engaging as a reflective practitioner is a deliberate act of integrating
the professional identity through one's conduct.

As university faculty, even at a teaching university, we are
encouraged and expected to engage in research. The research
follows our professional interests and, in an indirect way, supports the Mentor Leader group. One Mentor Leader continually
examines her relationship with her cohort groups, questioning

which practices shape her teacher candidates as reflective practitioners. She extends her research to integrate cohort student responses and evaluations of her work; she considers how their evaluations give weight to her classroom practice; and she makes deliberate choices about continued practice. In employing a "deliberate code of conduct," she may choose to reject a teacher candidate's suggestion for improvement if it substantially compromises her model of quality, inquiry-based education, or her ethics. While Mentor Leaders may shift in the method and possible models of teaching practices, we discourage change that perjures our professional identities.

Individual inquiry research and cohort evaluations do allow for a measure of self-inquiry among the Mentor Leaders. In addition, we participate in self-selected committees. We form these committees grounded in research, ethical questions, and reflective practice. For example, a question was recently posted on our Mentor Leader listserv regarding whether Mentor Leaders should evaluate how well our host teachers, the clinical faculty who are hosting teacher candidates in P–12 classroom placements, are doing in assisting in the preparation of teacher candidates. (The listserv augments our regular meetings by increasing communication and potentially diminishing isolation of new Mentor Leaders.) Strong, professionally informed opinions were posted in response to the question. The conversation that ensued at a subsequent Mentor Leader meeting helped to shape an ad hoc committee that will examine how teacher candidates are placed with host teachers. These conversations and problem-solving models serve to inform our reflective practice. "The development of knowledge and theories necessary for professional practice in the educational setting requires a willingness and capacity on the part of the teachers to 'problematize' practice, reflect and think critically about their practices in specific contexts" (Walkington, Christensen, and Kock 2001, 68).

In addition to problematizing practice, the listserv has become a place where we communicate our understandings of accreditation standards, the procedures to which we have agreed to employ, and any difficulties we seem to be encountering. Again, the conversation on the listserv comes to the Mentor

Leader meetings. In the past few years, a school-based committee that included P–12 faculty developed a rubric that would
support an inquiry-based integrative cohort program and would
meet the new teacher standards developed by the Interstate
New Teacher Assessment and Support Consortium (INTASC)
(1992). The rubric was modified based on feedback from Mentor
Leaders who must employ the rubric. Now the rubric, in its second year of use, will again be examined for its effectiveness as a
tool to determine in what ways our teacher candidates are developing as new teachers and reflective practitioners. The Mentor Leaders are not required to participate on the committee;
they do not receive any particular university credit for doing so,
except as service to the department and/or the school. Yet, we
understand the feedback as critical in shaping our programs and
our students. Mentor Leaders willingly serve on such committees, as it helps them to examine their personal beliefs, which can
help to develop the professional "I."

Layered onto regular meetings and the self-selected committees is participation in the teacher education profession and professional development. Each Mentor Leader gives presentations
and workshops at regional and national conferences. Some presentations are disciplinary specific (middle grades, special education, science education, etc.), yet each has the theoretic
underpinning of the field-based cohort program that we have
developed. We value and understand how our inquiry-based
practices are integrated into each aspect of our education model,
regardless of disciplinary focus. This is the strength whereby academics from disparate content expertise can develop both individually and collectively. The Mentor Leader group serves to
diminish Coles' (1997) barriers to reflective practice: "external
structures imposed by schools and school systems, the profession, governments, and the public at large" and "internal structures of anxiety, fear, loneliness, meaninglessness, helplessness,
and hostility" (10). We are committed to the Mentor Leader
group as it provides the location to examine our integrative practices. The better able we are to become reflective practitioners,
inquiring into sound practice and integrating our professional
identities into ethical teaching, the more easily we can help

teacher candidates become reflective practitioners, engaged in their profession and willing to work with unique problems of teaching (Kosnik 2001; Larrivee 2000; Whitehead 2000; McLaughlin 1999).

Inquiry Supporting Reflectivity

Most teacher candidates who come to. our program fit the national norms for many teacher education programs: European American, middle class, female, young twenties, healthy, moderate to great academic success. Most of these young women want, if not expect, to teach P–12 students who are like them. These typical candidates have not necessarily had their teaching beliefs challenged. Our program is meant to help teacher candidates interrogate assumptions. We have found out that forced critical attention to unexamined judgments helps teacher candidates to develop a teacher voice founded in critical inquiry and a teaching identity with a sense of agency (McLaughlin 1999). Throughout the two-year, field-based cohort program, teacher candidates are required to participate in focused writing that lifts up critical reflection as the highest attainment. Candidates are supported with feedback from the Mentor Leader throughout the semesters as they seek to attain critical reflection.

Teacher candidates are introduced to critical reflection in their first semester through dialectic journal writing and action research/inquiry projects. In an integrated science class, taken by teacher candidates from various disciplines, students receive feedback on their journals, which encourages them to move from contextual and dialogic writing toward dialectic. Contextual writing embodies basic technical interpretations, such as summary of texts or observed actions in field placements. Contextual writing is often where teacher candidates start. They list those things that are outside of themselves, with little obligation to explain the relevance of their observations. Once a candidate explains the importance of her observations in relationship to what is being learned in the university classrooms, to learning theory, to child development, and so on, the journal is then evaluated as dialogic. Dialogic writing carries with it the significance of making the bridge between observation and critique. Dialogic writing, however, still does not carry the reflective turn. Reflection is evident, but it is not enough to support the development of the "I" or, eventually, the reflective practice. Mentor Leaders continue to give feedback to support teacher candidates toward the dialectic rating—writing that not only offers critique but examines the assumptions and expectations embedded in the critique. There is often a struggle on the part of the teacher candidates to understand this progression and on the part of the Mentor Leader to give meaningful feedback to assist in the process.

Also in the first semester, teacher candidates are introduced to action research as a form of inquiry. Action research has been named many things—teacher research, classroom-based research, and so on—but it maintains essential elements of a question rooted in learning, a planned method of inquiry, collection of data (usually classroom observation), analysis, and interpretation. Within classroom-based action research, interpretation most often takes on the role of "solutions" to the examined learning problems. It is in this framework that we introduce action research to our teacher candidates. With the support of a course, teacher candidates identify their own burning questions, usually a disjuncture between what they think learning should be and what they are seeing in field placements. While new to the teacher's side of the desk, questions often center on student behavior. At this point, the teacher candidate's "I" is proscribed by management issues, the skills and strategies necessary to create an effective learning environment. Again, this positioning is evidence of a technical orientation, a low level of reflectivity as it relates to learning.

From the first semester to last, teacher candidates replicate pieces of the classroom-based action research in other coursework. In their final semester, they conduct an independent inquiry project for a "capstone" experience. The expectation is that the teacher candidate has developed an "I" that is self-aware enough to carry out critical examination through the tools of inquiry appropriate to teacher education and her own content disciplines. The teacher candidate chooses deliberate actions for unique problems and examines the results in the context of student learning. Action research, if it remains an academic exercise—done for courses and the university—has the potential to remain as what the teacher candidate believes about learning rather than what she knows and how she acts upon that knowledge. To help teacher candidates develop an accepted practice (praxis) that is necessary to become a reflective practitioner, we require a critical examination of their teaching (Korthagen and Kessels 1999).

Recently, we have shifted from teacher candidates' creating and teaching units in their senior year of field placements to completing teacher work samples. Even in action research we risk the possibility of reifying our unexamined beliefs (Argyris 1990). In a teacher work sample, teacher candidates are called on to show evidence of student learning, to examine contextual variables, and plan further instruction that would bring all students to higher levels of learning adequate to support their continued success in public schools. In expecting teacher candidates to examine, account for, and further consider student learning, we are engaging them to be reflective practitioners. With Mentor Leader support, it is hoped they learn to "act with integrity, openness, and commitment rather than compromise, defensiveness, or fear" (Larrivee 2000).

Inquiry Supporting Collaboration

As with many teacher education programs, we are grounded in social constructivist theory, as supported by Vygotsky's work. The extension of Schön's work into *Educating the Reflective Practitioner* (1987) aligns with Vygotsky's scaffolding model. We believe that the inquiry processes within our field-based program are carried out with the support of more able peers, whether we are considering mentor-to-mentor or modeling with teacher candidates in our classrooms.

Mentor Leaders have many opportunities to support each other. Not only do we regularly meet to discuss general and specific problems, we teach for one another's cohort, according to our academic expertise. Someone with a background of middle level education would teach the curriculum class for all middle grade cohorts, including her own. So she would plan courses, time to teach, and general content in concert with the cohort's Mentor Leader. Quite often, new Mentor Leaders co-teach some of their courses with more seasoned Mentor Leaders. In the close teaching environment created, we are challenged to model our "values in action" (Senge, Kleiner, Roberts, Ross, and Smith 1994).

In any profession, people are challenged to "do" as they "say." For our program, among the Mentor Leaders, we feel obligated to examine our own practice under the same inquiry-based integrative model that we employ with our teacher candidates. When the Mentor Leaders willingly engage in reflective practice, we are adopting a "programmatic stance" to help teacher candidates "acquire the skills and attitudes of reflective practitioners and learn to reflect in practice" (Kosnik 2001, 68). Most of that reflection is informal, both individual and collective. The Mentor Leader group comes back into the reflection process at this point as a crucible for examination. While we do have a regular, formal meeting of the group, we also hold informal consultations. The close teaching within our program provides for many moments of inquiry and discussion. This integrative model is an opportunity to explore possibilities with more able peers and colleagues. Our conversations invite us to inquire "in greater depth without reducing all questions of educational value to technical accounts of skill, competence and other measures of performance" (Rowland 2000).

Again, the Mentor Leader group becomes a model for teacher candidates from which we support collaboration. Mentor Leaders engage their cohorts in collaborative practices in classes as well as individually. One of the first classes a new cohort student takes is an integrated science class with cross-disciplinary representation in the instructors and the class participants. The science lessons are inquiry-based and the students are grouped to provide cross-collaboration among middle grades, early childhood, and special education cohorts (the same makeup of academic expertise in the Mentor Leader group). Within the "identification interdepartmental groups," as they are called, teacher candidates are expected to examine their understandings of new material with their peers. The inquiry-based lessons are designed so the participants cannot reduce the questions to matters of discrete skill or individual performance. Individuals are required to support one another in developing coherent explanations for scientific phenomena based on individual and collective planned observations.

With their Mentor Leaders, teacher candidates meet and participate in goal setting for individual development. The cohort student identifies an area of practice that he wishes to examine. The INTASC standards-based rubric (described previously) becomes the basis for evaluation. Teacher candidates reflect on their own levels of effective practice and determine either a formal or informal course of inquiry that would provide for reflection in action. The inquiry is developed with the more able guidance of the Mentor Leader and becomes one of the measures used to decide if a teacher candidate is making satisfactory progress in her program of study. In an inquiry-based program, the program of study combines designated courses with university and field-based experiences. As in the Mentor Leader group, teacher candidates are expected to question the status quo, become a perpetual problem solver who synthesizes experiences. In the goal-setting and subsequent feedback sessions, teacher candidates are asked to uncover underlying assumptions about teaching and learning, as well as indicate any new meanings they may have derived from the reflective process.

In keeping with collaboration with a more able peer, teacher candidates are also required to videotape their microteaching. This is a rather standard technique for individual review and reflection; however, in our program, a cohort peer must review the tape, giving critical feedback to the teaching peer. The intent is that the cohort student must articulate his professional "I" (even though it is still developing and finding its own voice) in order to determine the degree to which the teaching peer displays effective practice—that is, the degree to which the teaching peer can substantiate a deliberate code of conduct that is supportive of student learning. Just as the Mentor Leaders help one another to question teaching practices, cohort peers are expected to engage in like conversations. The engagement is modeled from Mentor Leader to Mentor Leader, from Mentor Leader to teacher candidate, and from candidate to candidate. One of our hopes is that the teacher candidate will become used to this pattern of reflection on action and will engage in similar practices once she has graduated from our program.

As Mentor Leaders engage in service to the department and university, teacher candidates are required to engage in service learning projects. Service learning has been broadly defined in recent research; we, however, prescribe two types of service learning: one that enriches their personal and professional lives and one that models service learning to their P–12 students. In the first type, teacher candidates are serving in required practica that bring them in contact with P–12 students for twelve to twenty hours per week. In their practica, the teacher candidates are expected to employ a code of conduct that will support the public learning environments, attend to the individual learning of all students, and develop their personal sense of the professional "I." The practica become locations where teacher candidates examine how their professional choices have an impact on P–12 students. While this practice describes many field-based models, we believe that the reflective turn required for our teacher candidates changes the dynamic so that teacher candidates are serving in a professional capacity, making professional decisions, and learning to critique their practice in what Schön would describe as "reflection on action."

Reflection on action describes the transitory moment of teaching where the individual makes decisions in concert with her code of conduct within the crucible of classroom teaching. Reflection on action requires that the individual comes to any problem solving with an articulated understanding of her pedagogical philosophy (Spilkova 2001). These types of external requirements can become normative for the teacher candidates if the Mentor Leader is not explicit in modeling reflection on action. Developing the professional "I" with teacher candidates should support "self-reflection on permanent critical investigation of one's own activity, on the readiness to discover problems, [and] on the ability permanently to ask new questions" (Spilkova 2001).

The second type of service learning required of teacher candidates mimics the service learning modeled between Mentor Leader and teacher candidate. The teacher candidates are expected to develop and support service-learning opportunities for their P–12 students. The intention is to employ a code of conduct that will support critical thinking with children. Mentor Leaders use practices that can be replicated and examined from the university setting to the public school setting. Explicit discussions with and high expectations of teacher candidates require that cohort students develop beyond rudimentary reflective practices that may or may not critically develop their professional "I" (Zeichner 1994).

Inquiry Supporting Commitment to Teaching and Learning

The professional educator who has a commitment to teaching and learning exhibits aspects of reflective practice: both reflection in action and reflection on action. The two aspects occur in two points in relationship to an educator's practice. Reflection in action occurs in the moment of practice. The practitioner adheres to his or her examined code of conduct and responds to unique problems the moment the problem presents itself. Reflection on action occurs as an antecedent to an event. Reflection on action has the potential of informing and shaping the professional "I," while reflection *in* action should be how the "I" negotiates unique problems. Reflection on action has a way of shaping professional identity and potentially contributes to the professional knowledge of education (Connelly and Clandinin 1990) because the professional educator is deliberately examining how his practice might improve.

Once the professional educator engages in reflection on action, she is moving toward establishing "living educational theories" (Whitehead 2000). Mentor Leaders, like any other academic in higher education, are at risk for becoming one who "professes" her beliefs about teaching and learning, rather than living and modeling her practice (Larrivee 2000; Spilkova 2001). In addition, most universities (for purposes of tenure and promotion) do not support a type of inquiry/research that examines the self in relationship to teaching and learning practice. For just those reasons, it is imperative to the Mentor Leaders that we have an ethic of collaboration, that we deliberately examine our practice in relationship to the learning of our teacher candidates, and that we continue to rely upon our critical practice as the educational standards for teaching and learning in our programs.

An ethic of collaboration, discussed elaborately in chapter 2, underpins our social constructivist and critical pedagogies of learning. As a Mentor Leader group and as individual reflective practitioners, we believe that one potential for learning is harbored within collaborative efforts. While our field-based cohort program is grounded in educational theory, its uniqueness sprung from the collaborative efforts of the mentors. As some mentors leave the university and others join, the program continues to shift to encompass the informed research of the new members while inducting them into the practices of the group. The change is positive in that it helps us to reflect continually upon our teaching practices.

Individual definitions of learning both broaden across the group and become more precise to the practices we use in our own classrooms. The writing of this book is an act of reflection on action, as the authors struggle to articulate what we know about teaching and learning and why the Mentor Leader group has served a specific function for our continued development as reflective practitioners. Our field-based program, like many teacher education programs, is subject to national standards and accrediting agencies. Again, the Mentor Leader group serves as a location where we examine the language of standards to determine how the learning of our teacher candidates meets or exceeds recommended criteria for effective practice.

In addition to the group, co-teaching of our courses allows us to observe one another's practice in action. In planning for classes, we are often forced to articulate why we think one activity rather than another will further support our teacher candidates' learning. When we cannot co-teach classes, we often collaborate on the development of courses. For example, two cohorts attending classes on different campuses would follow the same program of study for middle grades teacher candidates. So both classes would need the Ethics, Professionalism, and School Law classes in the same semester, delivered at two sites. In a recent semester, two Mentor Leaders taught the class; however, they planned the semester to maximize learning opportunities for both cohorts and integrated cross-cohort lessons that required collaborative work between two groups. Each professor took opportunities for reflection in action while teaching her class, but they also practiced reflection on action by consulting with each other, refining lessons for the classes, and developing activity assessments.

Our commitment to the Mentor Leader group and inquiry as reflective practice becomes the educational standard for all Mentor Leaders. This particular form of action research establishes its own norms, which are in conflict with the technical rationality supported by those who profess their beliefs, rather than live their beliefs (Schön 1983; Larrivee 2000). The norms encompass "open-mindedness, responsibility, and whole-heartedness," which are founded in the five phases of a Deweyian reflective cycle (Loughran 1996). Language to discretely describe the norms remains stubbornly elusive as they are interwoven with how we "know" and how our "knowing in action" supports the standards of our reflection in action. "The educational standards of reflective practitioners differ from traditional, 'linguistic' standards [in that] the living standards are embodied in the lives of practitioners and require ostensive definition to communicate their meanings" (Whitehead 2000, 99). As Mentor Leaders, we acknowledge that we are teachers, but we don't necessarily subscribe to static definitions of teaching. We choose to settle our educational standards in the shifting development of our professional "I," which is most critically seen in the learning of our teacher candidates.

Communicating these types of professional standards and norms to teacher candidates is a difficult task, one that continually challenges the Mentor Leader group. Engaging preservice teachers with reflection on action is quite the norm of teacher education programs theses days: journals, responses to lessons, peer-to-peer observation, portfolios, standards-based assessments—all, parts, and hybrids of these tools are found where academics support writing to learn theories. Our field-based cohort program is designed with extensive field experiences.

We consider the program to be a four-semester sequence. In the first three semesters, teacher candidates experience various school contexts and multiple grade levels under the supervision of selected host teachers. By the time teacher candidates are ready for their internship (called "student teaching" by many university programs), they have experienced seven hundred hours of public school teaching. Our teacher candidates begin microteaching and planning/teaching full-period lessons early in their first semester. This allows Mentor Leaders to observe teacher candidates' reflection in action.

In addition to extensive field experiences, our program of study integrates a capstone experience in the final semester. The capstone experience is broad-based action research, designed by each teacher candidate. The inquiry-oriented work is rooted in their practice and the learning of P–12 students. The teacher candidates consider the impact of their planned and "of the moment" choices for learners just as the Mentor Leaders do.

Conclusion

Throughout this chapter I have considered inquiry and reflective practice as the vehicles we use to promote integration of learning. As Mentor Leaders, we promote self-awareness, self-inquiry, and self-reflection. Personal beliefs about teaching, learning, and development inform our teaching and management decisions. Yet we acknowledge that any individual experience base has the potential for distorting the "norms" needed to promote the professional "I." A deep examination of closely held beliefs embodied in our assumptions about students and expectations determines critical reflection as an ongoing discovery for our reflection on action. While we collaborate with the Mentor Leader group, we also support individual growth to become perpetual problem solvers (reflection in action). We question the status quo, synthesizing experiences, integrating information and feedback, and uncovering underlying values to discover new meaning.

References

Argyris, C. 1990. *Overcoming organizational defenses: Facilitating organizational learning.* Boston: Allyn & Bacon.

Coles, A. 1997. Impediments to reflective practice: Toward a new agenda for research on teaching. *Teachers and Teaching: Theory and Practice* 3(1): 7–27.

Connelly, F. M., and J. Clandinin. 1990. Stories of experience and narrative inquiry. *Educational Researcher* 5: 2–14.

Interstate New Teacher Assessment and Support Consortium. 1992. *Model standards for beginning teacher licensing and development: A resource for state dialogue.* Washington, DC: Council of Chief State School Officers.

Kleine, K. L. M. 2000. Teaching for rationality: What does it mean for preservice middle level teachers' intellectual development? Ph.D. diss., University of Maine.

Korthagen, F. A. J., and J. P. A. M. Kessels. 1999. Linking theory and practice: Changing the pedagogy of teacher education. *Educational Researcher* 28(4): 4–17.

Kosnik, C. 2001. The effects of an inquiry-oriented teacher education program on a faculty member: Some critical incidents and my journey. *Reflective Practice* 2(1): 65–80.

Larrivee, B. 2000. Transforming teaching practice: Becoming the critically reflective teacher. *Reflective Practice* 1(3): 293–307.

Loughran, J. 1996. *Developing reflective practice: Learning about teaching and learning through modeling.* London: Falmer.

Mayhew, K. C., and A. C. Edwards. 1936/1966. *The Dewey school: The laboratory school of the University of Chicago, 1896–1903.* Introduction by J. Dewey. New York: Atherton Press.

McLaughlin, T. H. 1999. Beyond the reflective teacher. *Educational Philosophy and Theory* 31(1): 9–25.

Rowland, S. 2000. *The enquiring university teacher.* Buckingham, England: The Society for Research into Higher Education and Open University Press.

Schön, D. A. 1991. *The reflective turn: Case studies on educational practice.* New York: Teachers College.

Schön, D. A. 1987. *Educating the reflective practitioner: Toward a new design for teaching and learning in the professions.* San Francisco, CA: Jossey-Bass.

Schön, D. A. 1983. *The reflective practitioner: How professionals think in action.* New York: Basic Books.

Senge, P. M., A. Kleiner, C. Roberts, R. B. Ross, and B. J. Smith. 1994. *The fifth discipline fieldbook.* New York: Currency Doubleday.

Spilkova, V. 2001. Professional development of teachers and student teachers through reflection on practice. *European Journal of Teacher Education* 24(1): 59–65.

Walkington, J., H. P. Christensen, and H. Kock. 2001. Developing critical reflection as a part of teaching training and teaching practice. *European Journal of Engineering Education* 26(4): 343–50.

Whitehead, J. 2000. How do I improve my practice? Creating and legitimating an epistemology of practice. *Reflective Practice* 1(1): 91–104.

Zeichner, K. 1994. Research on teacher thinking and different views of reflective practice in teaching and teacher education. In *Teachers' minds and action: Research on teachers' thinking and practice,* edited by I. Carlgren, G. Handal, and S. Vaage. London: Falmer Press.

5

Learning to Foster and Provoke Uncertainty, Ambiguity, and Change

Karynne L. M. Kleine

> Change means movement. Movement means friction. Only in the frictionless vacuum of a nonexistent abstract world can movement or change occur without that abrasive friction of conflict.
>
> —Saul Alinsky, "The Purpose,"
> *Rules for Radicals* (1971)

In our inquiry (chapter 4), we understand for change to occur we must face uncertainty and ambiguity. We have recognized this as central to our accomplishments (chapter 5).

Why We Have Learned to Foster the Management of Change

In these times of focus on school reform, in what may sometimes seem like dizzying change, it is prudent that we consult findings from organizational theory because a large body of research on organizational change has already been developed. "Organizations by their very nature are conservative" (Hall 1999). Thus, in times of flux, organizations will attempt to maintain footing, which could lead to a clash due to the opposing desired outcomes. Furthermore, just as organizations behave in ways that resist change, so do the people within them.

In particular, P–16 schools, the organizations of which we find ourselves largely a part, are institutions that counter change (Glickman 1993). Change itself is inevitable, although the manner and kind of change are variable. Thus, when change is to be expected, the response of some educators is to act as if it will not come. Possibly because of a need to avoid dissonance and maintain the status quo and their core beliefs, people impose a clarity and a certainty that are not actually there. For the most part, educators have learned to impose this certainty and clarity on those indeterminate environments because of a thorough grounding in technical rationality, the lowest level of reflectivity (Van Manen 1977; see chapter 4). This causes them to focus on "the means rather than the ends" and to act as though there was only one meaning, one possible outcome, to pursue (226). Then, when faced with a decision that must be made or an interpretation that must be drawn in an uncertain, ambiguous environment, they revert to a process with which they are more comfortable to impose a moratorium on the problematic uncertainty. These actions are entirely understandable in light of the fact that organizations to which they have been so strongly enculturated need to maintain stability.

As products of especially conservative institutions, school of education faculty tend to have little experience making decisions in what are recognized by them as ambiguous, uncertain environments, preferring to adhere to contexts and decisions that are familiar. Thus, those in academia, a time-honored profession, have earned the reputation for staidness; they do not, as a general rule, chase opportunities as do personnel in fast-moving, private-sector corporations. These corporations, filled with graduates of professional business schools, are often held up as paragons of virtue in our society since they can respond so quickly to change. Yet, given the pace that all professionals today are expected to keep, professors especially need to know how to operate in environments of change. Products of a system that breeds technical rationality, school of education faculty often are not used to solving ill-structured problems, and our response to them is one of defensiveness and fear (Larrivee 2000; see chapter 4). Because of our inexperience, we are not confident in those situations that call for a decision, especially when the information is sketchy, complex, or overwhelming. Frequently these situations arise because there is no time to gather data or consult with others, as is true for those who work in hospital emergency rooms (McAninch 1993). Given that educators, in general, come from such a guarded milieu, it is more surprising that our professional community of Mentor Leaders has been able to cultivate a different approach to change. Our organization is a change agent (Hall 1999) having far-reaching effects.

In this chapter we will discuss another significant heuristic utilized by the Mentor Leaders, both in their professional community as well as with teacher candidates, to effect change and growth in education. One feature that stands out to us in the Mentor Leader group is the way we contend with, embrace, and even provoke uncertainty, ambiguity, and change in the teacher candidates and in ourselves. It is this feature that helps move the Mentor Leader into the role of professional, and the Mentor Leader group into a community of inquirers.

How Our Scholarship Fosters the Capacity to Operate in Uncertain, Ambiguous Environments

Scientists operate within communities of inquiries. These professional communities help the members shape the values and norms for their work (Latour 1987). In terms of scholarship, our work as a professional community is a type of design experiment, wherein we have attempted to identify useful learning strategies as they are implemented and then have tried to determine what makes them effective. Design experiments vary from traditional research in that understanding of a complex interrelationship, rather than causation, is sought. We have looked closely at what seems to make our professional community unique, successful, and most useful to our students as they learn to become professional educators. In this generative process we draw on our own critical thinking skills to analyze and continually refocus to see if, and how, transfer of learning is occurring. We try to make our tacit theories explicit as a means of scholarly endeavor.

Ironically, since we must make these close observations our-selves during what might be termed the "treatment" phase in a classical, controlled experiment, as well as its being dynamic and cyclical in nature, the theory we are describing is itself an in-stance of operating in an uncertain, tentative environment. Fur-thermore, since Mentor Leaders choose to be a part of a closely linked community, they must learn to accept the nonstandard-ization that characterizes professionals functioning in an un-predictable environment. Valuing this type of scholarship, as evidenced by the writing of this book, demonstrates that we rec-ognize that learning to deal with uncertain, ambiguous situa-tions is a necessary element of a professional community. How, then, do we learn to deal with ambiguity and uncertainty? What do these terms mean?

Definitions of Terms

Ambiguity is a term that has at least two meanings. One connota-tion is that there are multiple meanings of reality. This multiplicity can be due to language, representations, or the situation itself. For example, when a Mentor Leader relays to a colleague that a teacher candidate needs more experience listening to what children really mean, the Mentor Leader is indicating that the candidate is not paying attention to the multiple meanings of a word—that she makes a situation ambiguous by her language (or inattention to it). For instance, a teacher candidate was teaching a science lesson on phases of matter but kept using the term "states" of matter. The children related it to the United States, misunderstanding those fifty units as a synonym for "phases," and the teacher candidate re-inforced a misconception because she didn't anticipate multiple meanings of the word. Further, with so many variables at play in a complex place such as a classroom, which could make the mean-ing of nearly anything ambiguous, she didn't perceive that this (mis)learning had taken place.

The other dimension of ambiguity is that there is awareness that everything acted upon is tentative. It is a stance one takes regarding evidence. Ambiguity is object-oriented—for example, "The situation is ambiguous." This dimension speaks to the fact that one cannot know for sure what evidence will be convincing until gathered. This is the pragmatists' sense that "the truth is told" in the action. Plausibility and possibility become important to gauge. Evidenced-based reasoning, as a disposition and a practice, become key. Developing this habit of mind for looking ahead and anticipating consequences as a core belief (Gess-Newsome 2003) is what seems to separate those who can dwell in an ambiguous environment as opposed to those who tend to avoid it.

Uncertainty has to do with the outcome; we cannot know how something will turn out in advance—regardless of how much we would like to know. Uncertainty is increased as the environment changes because problems become less defined and important information becomes harder to discern. Of course, if we are observant, outcomes can be categorized as being of degrees of certainty—more or less certain—rather than absolutes. Uncertainty is subject-oriented—for example, "I am uncertain especially because of the ambiguous situation." Often with uncertainty there is more information in a situation than will pertain to the solution/resolution. This can be a distracter for the decision maker.

Connections and Capsulations

One aspect of scientific knowledge is the awareness that it is tentative (Schwartz and Lederman 2002). "Tentative" here doesn't mean necessarily that the knowledge is unstable and therefore untrustworthy, but rather there is an acknowledgement that new data, or a new framework for interpreting the data, may come to light and change an existing understanding. For answering particular types of questions, this scientific way of viewing the world is an indispensable characteristic. It seems to follow that for those who have a certain orientation toward uncertainty and ambiguity, tentativeness is valued and affirmed, rather than evaded. This whole process of dwelling well with uncertain, ambiguous environments and therefore recognizing tentativeness could be called the "experimental attitude" as advocated by Dewey.

Attitudes that Dewey (1933) stated were necessary for intelligent thought include open-mindedness, wholeheartedness, and responsibility. While all three are necessary, it is the last one that is most important; it is used to draw attention to the importance of remaining responsive and responsible to the full consequences of inquiry. Responsibility, usually understood as a moral trait, is rarely seen as an intellectual resource; it is the attitude that ensures that consequences will be considered, thus separating the intelligent thinker from the believer. At any point, obstructing the process forecloses reflective thinking. Learning to accept uncertainty, ambiguity, and tentativeness as inherent to successful inquiry is a focus of our professional group because of the poor outcomes that stem from foreclosing reflective thinking.

Reflective thinkers operate with a give-and-take between what is given and what is inferred. They recognize the need to remain in touch with both facts and ideas (Dewey 1933). King and Kitchener (1994) note that those able to reflect at the highest level recognize that any solution is one's best conjecture of "what is." Less reflective individuals rush in to resolve disequilibria, at times because they are uncomfortable with the doubt required by the tentative balancing of facts and ideas. This desire for surety leads to a technical orientation suggestive of the amateur rather than the professional. Because we value reflective practices, ease and facility in contending with ambiguity, uncertainty, and tentativeness are necessary components to developing professionalism. It is through this we learn to accept change, and it is from this that true change is effected.

Complex Nature Ensures Uncertainty and Ambiguity

Mentor Leaders working with their first cohort will attest that, while there are resources available for use, there is almost always a nagging feeling that accompanies every decision as to whether it "is right." Sometimes the decision is whether to gently nudge a teacher candidate, push him hard and ask others to assist, or leave him alone. Sometimes it is whether to schedule math class in the morning or afternoon. At other times it is deciding how to try to motivate, or whether to motivate, a very tired cohort. Often these decisions need to be made in a dynamic, quick-paced environment.

The need for "being right" is probably part of human nature. Therefore, good Mentor Leaders carry sensors in their heads that are continually discerning the variables impinging on a situation, and they utilize a sophisticated weighing machine that triggers itself when a decision needs to be made. This portrayal of the process of data awareness and gathering to inform decision making sounds very much like the skills one would find on the resume of a critical thinker. However, even with the development of these advanced managerial sensors, Mentor Leaders employ strategies to help them deal with the nagging feelings that are part and parcel of the decision-making process. Many times we've said to new Mentor Leaders—after listening to their concerns, making suggestions, and directing them to the handbook—that there really is no instruction manual that supplements the job. What we do try to do in place of an instruction manual is model and explicate our dispositions as well as help them acquire a language to express the concepts they are forming. The Mentor Leader listserv offers many examples of how this is done.

The Mentor Leader listserv has developed as a communication tool. Because not all members are on one campus and because the views of all were frequently needed when making decisions, Mentor Leaders, as one of their first tasks, are asked to subscribe and contribute to the conversations on the listserv. Veteran members submit questions, asking others to respond. This often spurs discussion or offerings of experiences. The tone of the "guidance" is often gentle, with multiple, and at times different, responses presented. None of these is generally considered to be "right," but there is an acceptance that "not knowing" and taking time to judge is an acceptable approach to problem solving. In this way new members come to see what are acceptable ways to respond to situations as well as to others.

How experienced members help new members learn to operate in uncertain, ambiguous environments can be illustrated by
how the listserv is used to set the agenda for an upcoming meeting. Often a veteran Mentor Leader will take the lead by setting
the date for an initial group meeting and sending a message asking for items for the agenda. She then takes responsibility for
compiling the items, allotting time for each item, and often acting
as a facilitator at the meeting. These responsibilities are not assigned, and new members see that veterans take on the task without being asked. The veterans are modeling for new members the
expectation for membership—being self-directed, anticipatory,
and proactive. They also model types of questions and responses
appropriate for the listserv.

From time to time an individual has a question best addressed to another individual, but it gets sent to the list. Shortly
thereafter a message to remind those on the list that the "reply"
feature results in everyone on the list receiving the message
will appear. This type of response reminds participants to be
cognizant of communication "rules." It also demonstrates that
members see one of their roles as instructing newer members of
the community to the community values and norms in a non-
threatening manner. The importance of the use of tactful language is also part of what veterans convey. It is typical to see that
in a short period of time new Mentor Leaders begin to adopt the
roles of facilitators, learning to offer to contribute without being
asked.

We recognize that being a Mentor Leader is no different than
any leadership position that requires a great deal of coordination
of efforts and judgment (Hall 1999). By nature the position is full
of uncertainty and ambiguity. Certainly CEOs and presidents
give each other tips on how to perform the job successfully, and
certainly many have been through an MBA or similar training
program; but because each context, each situation, and each per-
sonality varies from another, there is judgment inherent in any
decision that renders it distinctive. Acknowledging this element
is essential for being a critical thinker. More importantly, a phase
that precedes the actual decision making is having a particular
disposition toward it. This disposition closely aligns with risk

taking. Martinello and Cook (1994) note that having the desire and ability to subject patterns one sees to criticism is the hallmark of an expert inquirer. They further note that any inquiry carried out with enthusiasm and care is the same process used by experts in a field.

Moreover, Dewey (1933) proposes that thinking only begins in ambiguous situations that present a dilemma; the state of perplexity starts the process of inquiry. However, this alone is not enough: "One can think reflectively only when one is willing to endure suspense and undergo the trouble of searching" (16). Dewey adds that to be considered "reflective thinking," the ideas that occur must be critiqued, and he notes that shortening the process by jumping to the first satisfactory conclusion is better described as "bad thinking" (16). Having the desire and ability to endure the protracted state of doubt and engage one's intellect is required of the critical thinker.

It is perhaps here that the professional community has the most influence on those uncomfortable or inexperienced with uncertainty, ambiguity, and change. As a group, we tend to view this state as positive, as an opportunity, rather than an obstacle to avoid. This receptive treatment comes as a result of a developed sense of "I," which Whitehead (2000) suggests is a way of holding together two mutually exclusive values—that is, to be comfortable with a situation that naturally produces discomfort. Parker Palmer (1998), in his book that advocates being introspective about teaching, maintains that it is from the identity and integrity of the teacher that good teaching can be found. He refers to these opposites as a part of "the hidden wholeness—paradoxes in teaching and learning" (61). Palmer notes the negative effects of adopting an "either-or" stance about teaching and learning, and he proposes that fragmented analysis destroys the possibility for finding connectedness. Given the tendency for academics to "think the world apart" (62), perhaps most remarkable of the Mentor Leader professional community is our success in teaching this form of integration to others.

Many beginning Mentor Leaders tend to avoid conflict, probably due to their socialization as teachers and, frequently, their experiences as the less dominant sex (Hargreaves 1994).

Many are used to bending to authority, often without questioning the legitimacy of the authority. This strategy, though disempowering at times, is often useful. After all, there is very little ambiguity in doing as one is told. However, the Mentor Leader group, begun and maintained without official administrative authorization, is less in the business of telling colleagues what to do and more in helping them embrace uncertainty and ambiguity (or at least recognize uncertainty and ambiguity) and make a choice in the face of such ambiguity.

When a first-year Mentor Leader, RP, expressed frustration and doubt at being able to execute the responsibilities of her job as effectively as others whom she is attempting to model, she sought counsel from another fairly inexperienced Mentor Leader, MA. RP, in a discombobulated rush to head out of the office, says, "I have to go to Black Elementary. How do y'all have time to see every student every week?" MA indicates that she initially felt the need to see every student with the same frequency and found the demands to be impossible. She asks RP to think about why is she going out to the school—to meet someone else's standard or to meet her own. RP decides that she is both trying to meet someone else's supposed expectation as well as her assumption that the students desire to have frequent contact. MA asks RP to explain how she thinks this is helpful for herself and/or the teacher candidate. Eventually RP decides that running herself ragged is not in her own best interest and is creating dependency in the teacher candidates. She keeps the appointment for that day but later explains to her cohort that she is purposefully not making herself available to solve their problems. She begins to be more deliberate about how she spends her limited time.

This case is illustrative about how Mentor Leaders help to socialize others so that they see themselves as capable. Here the beginning Mentor Leader, JM, is developing Whitehead's (2000) "I," a living contradiction (see chapter 4). She is learning how to be accessible to students while at the same time not enabling them. This balance is an extremely delicate one, but it is one that Jane seems intent upon cultivating. She also seems relieved that, while she has models, she is not expected to be like any other Mentor Leader.

Because Mentor Leaders are ultimately responsible for guiding teacher candidates to be thriving, effective inservice teachers, a heady responsibility, excellent individual and collective decision-making skills are crucial for their success. Requisite for developing those skills is recognizing and dealing with uncertainty, ambiguity, and change. In other words, if an educator faced with a complex situation was taught to reduce it to a single dimension so as to cancel out the uncertainty and ambiguity inherent in it as do those with a technical orientation, that would be an insufficient and undesirable outcome for a professional education program (Schön 1983). The way around developing a technical orientation is creating an environment for supportive autonomy (Reeve 1999). The Mentor Leader group functions to assist individuals in defining themselves as capable. This comes about because people in the group actually do develop capabilities, or it comes about because the group helps individuals recognize and name, at least privately, those capabilities.

The tendency to support autonomy as Reeve (1999) suggests is an interpersonal skill that assists others in developing intrinsic motivation. It can be considered a perspective on empowerment wherein power is shared with others rather than desired in order to act independently and have power over others (Irwin 1996). Not every Mentor Leader necessarily develops this interpersonal style and view of empowerment, but many do. A few, however, continue to look to parts of the professional community to reinforce and affirm a technical orientation.

Professionals are known for their ability not only to act independently but also to work cooperatively to maintain the integrity of the profession. There is a balance between individualism and collectivism. This would be another example of a living contradiction (Whitehead 2000). Our Mentor Leader group has evolved to serve both capacities at once. The structure now exists to provide supportive autonomy. Good Mentor Leaders turn to the group for modeling, advice, or opportunities to float ideas. This contribution is acknowledged. It may sound odd to define "taking from the group" as a contribution, but if the point of the group is to support the development of good Mentor Leaders, then this opportunity to offer support is a contribution. After using and contributing to the group in this way, the Mentor Leader can turn outward and attempt to solve her problem on her own. Though the situation she faces may be ambiguous, uncertain, or both, she has a greater capacity for acting tentatively, knowing this is the stance the group cultivates and values. In other words, with the experience of the group, the Mentor Leader becomes autonomous. Furthermore, he is encouraged to reflect on the outcome of the decision, to ascertain its validity, to be, as Dewey (1933) would say, a responsible thinker. Where this process breaks down is when Mentor Leaders don't use their growing capacity for autonomy to play a role in the development of other Mentor Leaders or when Mentor Leaders fail to develop the stance of tentativeness and openness to change required in the professional community.

Supportive autonomy is the mechanism by which energy is imported into the group to keep it functioning. It is also the mechanism that feeds and motivates individual Mentor Leaders as they contend with uncertainty and ambiguity. Often it is the means by which we learn how to go beyond a transmissive model of teaching and learning and trust in ourselves. The group may be functioning as a form of shelter for Mentor Leaders, or protracted think time, within which beliefs can be examined and possibly changed. Members are encouraged to utilize the group as a haven, not so much for protection from criticism, but as a place where deliberation is valued. This shelter enables Mentor Leaders to calculate and take risks they might otherwise be unwilling to take for fear of being wrong. In this way individuals learn how to be Mentor Leaders rather than merely learn how to do the work of a Mentor Leader. Characteristics of this professional community include members' making deliberate decisions and acting intentionally. This approach to inquiry matters far more than does a member's being "right," enabling Mentor Leaders to function more effectively in conditions of change.

This same stance of operating within the complexity, uncertainty, and ambiguity inherent in teaching is one that Mentor Leaders, to varying degrees and with varying degrees of success, promote with the teacher candidates. Most teacher candidates have had enough experience pondering teaching that they are dissatisfied with a technical orientation (Kleine 2000). Most feel they are well prepared for the intricacies that come under the heading "teaching" (JHL SoE assessment data, 2001), and our retention rate of over 90 percent in the field after three years supports this generalization. The most developed cohorts understand that uncertainty and ambiguity are not conditions to avoid. Indeed they learn that they are conditions that cannot be avoided.

One illustration of how Mentor Leaders use the support of the group to effect change with their cohorts can be seen in the reaction of teacher candidates to an assignment in a junior-level science class in fall 2000. The illustration also points out the significant role that communication among Mentor Leaders plays.

Three Mentor Leaders—one brand new, Maria; one with four years' experience, Karynne; and one with five years' experience (though significantly more as a professor), Sophie—were attempting to "team teach" the science course to three cohorts. The particular objective was to have the teacher candidates examine the differences between the ways the Japanese and American educational systems inculcate self-directed learning. The point of the exercise for teacher candidates was to note that the more self-directed learners score higher on science achievement than do the dependent learners, and to question the ways in which the American system promotes dependency. Teacher candidates were to read an article and respond to guided questions, which they then evaluated in small groups. Karynne, the Mentor Leader responsible for planning the activity, determined in consultation with the newest member of the trio, Maria, that the teacher candidates would not turn their papers in for further feedback from the professors. While this was communicated via e-mail to the veteran professor, Sophie, she never received the message and was unaware that the procedure would vary from the norm.

The assignment was conveyed to the teacher candidates later than usual, and many spent much time and effort word processing their responses, as that is what we had specified is acceptable presentation for professional work. Furthermore, several asked Karynne and Maria if they needed to spend time word processing and were told to turn in professional work, while others asked this question of Sophie and she replied, "Yes."

After the small-group discussions in class, Karynne moved on to the next activity. Immediately there was a flurry of hand-raising to indicate that the papers needed to be collected. Karynne informed the teacher candidates that since they had had feedback in the groups, it was unnecessary for the papers to be collected. The anger level in the room increased noticeably as many students realized that the professors would not know if they had spent time answering the questions well and, particularly, whether they had word processed their responses. Furthermore, Sophie was angry because she was unaware about the unusual procedure not to give the students credit for their work. Karynne was puzzled by this response, as she believed Sophie to have received the message.

Karynne, Maria, and several students pointed out how the activity was similar to one that might be used in Japan to inculcate self-directed learning. This did not appease many students who felt deceived because their efforts to learn would not be acknowledged by the professors.

In later analysis, some of it done with her own cohort, Karynne realized that the majority of the angry students were from the other two groups and that, overwhelmingly, teacher candidates in her cohort understood the point of the exercise and were satisfied with the level of feedback they had received. In fact they were as puzzled by the hostile response of the other cohorts as Karynne was. This cohort was definitely more comfortable not having the parameters spelled out to them and their efforts validated for following the specifications. This cohort, in contrast to the others, seemed to value substance over form. This cohort was learning that uncertainty and ambiguity are not conditions that should promote anger; rather, they are conditions that must be contended with by the effective teacher.

Further analysis of this incident shows that Karynne came into the group just as it was establishing its norms. Using the support of the group, she had come to adopt and practice the stance on operating in a changing environment. She had re-

ceived the "supportive autonomy" of the group and took calcu-
lated risks as a result. The group assisted Karynne in her professional development.

Contrastingly, Sophie, strongly socialized in another tradition and whose inclination was to remain connected to the
tightly scripted technical orientation that had made her successful as a teacher, did not utilize the group for such development.
She either couldn't, or wouldn't, draw on the group's support to
develop her autonomy, her risk taking, her willingness to challenge the technical orientation prevalent in teacher education
programs. It would take time before this would happen.

Uncertainty and Ambiguity in Critical Thinking

Many models of thinking—from Bloom's taxonomy to Cambourne's (1995) conditions for learning, to Wiggins and
McTighe's (1998) six facets of understanding—recognize that
some cognitive functions are more challenging than others. Each
of the models referred to here calls for circumspection to engage
in the more challenging types of thinking. In Bloom's taxonomy
these are the processes of analyzing, synthesizing, and evaluating. For Cambourne's model, the conditions that precede demanding cognitive processes are engagement, responsibility,
and approximation. The facets of understanding that require
complex processing are explanation, interpretation, application,
perspective, empathy, and self-knowledge. Each of these
processes, in addition to being challenging, also requires self-
direction to contend with the tentativeness inherent in each.
Dealing with uncertainty and ambiguity will be a part of the processing required for these abstract types of thinking. Thus, they
may be thought of as aspects of critical thinking.

Critical thinking has several elements. It relies on appropriate access to empirical knowledge in spite of the abstract nature
of premises. It is enhanced to the degree that the person is
trusted and seen as a capable professional (Nolan and Meister
2000). Real change represents a serious personal and collective
experience characterized by ambivalence and uncertainty, and it

results in a sense of mastery, accomplishment, and professional growth.

Popkewitz (2000) notes a shift since World War II emphasizing interdisciplinary knowledge with images of the teacher as problem solver. In looking at systems of reasoning, he sees a pattern of concern with how knowledge is socially constructed. These strands, which could be referred to as constructivism, all indicate a greater role for uncertainty and ambiguity for knowledge creation. Thus to be a critical thinker would entail one's being able to judge evidence in light of the situation.

To create a community of continuous inquiry entails a great degree of complexity and uncertainty (Cowan and Capers 2000). Communities need to be transparent (no hidden agendas), deliberate, and flexible. With continuous change, this stance and practice are no longer a luxury requiring education *for* uncertainty. Tolerance for, and coping comfortably with, ambiguity and risk taking can be learned, and it is a part of good decision making and problem solving. It seems to be an integral part of our community that by forming allegiances beyond the local, we learn this disposition. For inquiry, one should incorporate a respect for the messiness, uncertainty, and ambiguity that are a part of the process.

Relationship to Intellectual Development

Mentor Leaders come into the group with the expectation that they will be intelligent people; after all, each holds an advanced degree. However, they do not enter equally intellectually developed. Ability to dwell with uncertainty, ambiguity, and tentativeness is characteristic of the more intellectually developed; thus, it is this facility that will be purposefully engendered by participation in the group so that it can be fostered with the students. There is tension apparent—for instance, between special educators and their regular education counterparts—on how willing we are to dwell in the murkiness of abstraction. For instance, it seems that Mentor Leaders with a special education background do not find reflective thinking as compelling as do those from a regular education perspective, and we speculate that it has something to do with our use of principles of behaviorism, which are heavily utilized with many identified special learners. Sometimes our training or other experiences make us hesitant to suspend judgment and entertain doubt. The group functions in part to help Mentor Leaders change, if necessary, their conceptions of the effective guide from that of an authoritarian controller to an autonomous agent. With changed conceptions come changed behaviors.

As one refers back to the chapters of this book, a thread is woven throughout. The thread is intellectual development as defined in *Women's Ways of Knowing* (Belinky et al. 1986), wherein cognition and emotion are joined in the most advanced intellects. This intellectual coupling would represent how we go about teaching the integration of theory and practice. Furthermore, our community helps to enhance the intellect of each of our members, which in turn develops their sense of agency and empowerment. It also helps us recognize that awareness of relationships is information vital to informed decision making. Because one needs to accept and operate out of emerging situations, as is frequently the case for Mentor Leaders, dealing with uncertainty and ambiguity, as well as taking a tentative approach to knowledge, is also bound to intellectual development. It seems that by applying our intellects and understanding of a professional community, we have hit upon a very successful vehicle for contending with change and reforming education. We continue to become Mentor Leaders in a professional community.

An Illustration

Dee, Janice, and Karynne, experienced Mentor Leaders who co-teach a course on culture and language, gather around a table on a Tuesday evening. This is Karynne's first time through the venture that Dee and Janice have collaborated on for several iterations. They discuss their observations of the students' assuredness with regard to class discussions about racism and how the sense of finality expressed disturbs them. They trade anecdotes of their concerns, lightheartedly referring to the remarks of one such assured teacher candidate—"I'll just start my own business"—but the laughter doesn't mask their intent to have the teacher candidates confront their rigidity. At the meeting, seemingly everything is up for negotiation. It is not long before views and ideas are articulated, and the three collaborators have come up with a sequence of experiences and assignments to provoke uncertainty regarding positions on racism, to revolve around the theme "Outsider Within." Although it is midway through the course, the online syllabus and assignment guide are quickly revamped, and students are made aware of the changes at the next class meeting. Early data suggest that the sequence is successful; students seem to grasp the multiple dimensions of the issue. Dee, Janice, and Karynne continue to meet frequently to discuss the outcome of this decision and negotiate others, confident that they are challenging *and* supporting the students.

References

Alinsky, S. 1971. The purpose. In *Rules for radicals*. New York: Knopf.

Belinky, M. F., B. M. Clinchy, N. R. Goldberger, and J. M. Tarule. 1986. *Women's ways of knowing: The development of self, voice, and mind*. New York: Basic Books.

Cambourne, B. 1995. Toward an educational relevant theory of literacy learning. *Reading Teacher* 49(3): 182–90.

Cowan, D., and M. Capers. 2000. Co-developers: Partners in a study of professional learning communities. *Issues about Change* 8(2).

Dewey, J. 1933/1998. *How we think: A restatement of the relation of reflective thinking to the educative process*. Boston: Houghton Mifflin.

Gess-Newsome, J. 2003 (March). *Implications of the definitions of knowledge and beliefs on research and practice in science teacher education*. Paper presented at the Annual Meeting of the National Association for Research in Science Teaching, Philadelphia, PA.

Glickman, C. D. 1993. Restructuring policy for America's schools. *NASSP Bulletin* 76(549): 87–97.

Hall, R. H. 1999. *Organizations: Structures, processes, and outcomes*. 7th ed. Upper Saddle River, NJ: Prentice-Hall.

Hargreaves, A. 1994. *Changing teachers, changing times*. New York: Teachers College Press.

John H. Lounsbury School of Education. 2001. Assessment data reports.

King, P. M., and K. S. Kitchener. 1994. *Developing reflective judgment: Understanding and promoting intellectual growth and critical thinking in adolescents and adults.* San Francisco: Jossey-Bass.

Kleine, K. L. M. 2000. *Teaching for rationality: What does it mean for preservice middle level teachers' intellectual development?* Ph.D. diss., University of Maine.

Irwin, J. W. 1996. *Empowering ourselves and transforming schools: Educators making a difference.* Albany, NY: SUNY Press.

Larrivee, B. 2000. Transforming teaching practice: Becoming the critically reflective teacher. *Reflective Practice* 1(3): 293–307.

Latour, B. 1987. *Science in action: How to follow scientists and engineers through society.* Cambridge, MA: Harvard University Press.

Martinello, M. L., and G. E. Cook. 1994. *Interdisciplinary inquiry in teaching and learning.* New York: Macmillan College Publishing.

McAninch, A. R. 1993. *Teacher thinking and the case method: Theory and future directions.* New York: Teachers College Press.

Nolan, J., Jr., and D. Meister. 2000. *Teachers and educational change: The lived experience of secondary school restructuring.* Albany, NY: State University of New York Press.

Palmer, P. J. 1998. *The courage to teach: Exploring the inner landscape of a teacher's life.* San Francisco: Jossey-Bass.

Popkewitz, T. S. 2000. The denial of change in educational change: Systems of ideas in the construction of national policy and evaluation. *Educational Researcher* 29(1): 17–29.

Reeve, J. 1999. Autonomy-supportive teachers: How they teach and motivate students. *Journal of Educational Psychology* 91(3): 537–48.

Schön, D. A. 1983. *The reflective practitioner: How professionals think in action.* New York: Basic Books.

Schwartz, R. S., and N. G. Lederman. 2002. "It's the nature of the beast": The influence of knowledge and intentions on learning and teaching nature of science. *Journal of Research in Science Teaching* 39(3): 205–36.

Van Manen, M. 1977. Linking ways of knowing with ways of being practical. *Curriculum Inquiry* 6(3): 205–28.

Whitehead, J. 2000. How do I improve my practice? Creating and legitimating an epistemology of practice. *Reflective Practice* 1(1): 91–104.

Wiggins, G. P., and J. McTighe. 1998. *Understanding by design.* Alexandria, VA: Association for Supervision and Curriculum Development.

Index

About the Authors

Karynne L. M. Kleine is associate professor in the Department of Middle Grades Education at Georgia College & State University. She has settled in Georgia after a lifetime of moving through the states. Although she is a risk taker, she is happy to have landed among such great colleagues doing such important work.

Leigh Craft Hern is assistant professor in the Department of Middle Grades Education at Georgia College & State University. She has traveled all her life and for now is content to keep Georgia as her home base. She enjoys the challenging conversations her colleagues provide about her professional interests and theirs.

Nancy B. Mizelle is assistant professor in the Department of Early Childhood and Middle Grades Education at Georgia College & State University. She is a wife, a mother, a grandmother, and an educator.

Dee M. Russell is associate professor in the Department of Early Childhood Education at Georgia College & State University. He is the personal servant of a calico cat; in his free time, he follows his interests in curriculum for young children, the philosophy of John Dewey, and origami.

Cynthia J. Alby is associate professor in the Department of Foundations and Secondary Education at Georgia College & State University. She enjoys raising guide dog puppies for the blind, kayaking, biking, and settling into her new twenty-seven-acre farm. Her professional interests include diversity issues, the Belizean education system, and constructivism.

Victoria W. Hunnicutt is assistant professor in the Department of Early Childhood Education at Georgia College & State University. She enjoys living in the country with her husband, cat, and dog. She is a retired teacher and administrator who loves working with college students.